ARMED FORCES
ORIGAMI

JAYSON MERRILL

DOVER PUBLICATIONS, INC.
MINEOLA, NEW YORK

INTRODUCTION

With this book, folders will learn how to create 15 different models. The models are designed to perform a coordinated amphibious assault, and are designed to be functional. Ships will float, jets will fly, transformers will transform, and the missiles can be attached to various craft. I recommend using foil paper and then spray painting the finished models to waterproof them. A high skill level is needed in order to properly fold the models in this book, as they are very complex. I hope that you enjoy this book and building your own strike force!

Dedication

I dedicate this book to my daughters, Madda and Kk.

Bibliographical Note

Armed Forces Origami is a new work, first published by Dover Publications, Inc., in 2017.

Library of Congress Cataloging-in-Publication Data

Names: Merrill, Jayson, author.
Title: Armed forces origami / Jayson Merrill.
Description: Mineola, New York : Dover Publications, Inc., [2017]
Identifiers: LCCN 2017000034| ISBN 9780486815787 | ISBN 0486815781
Subjects: LCSH: Origami. | Weapons in art. | Military miniatures.
Classification: LCC TT872.5 .M469 2017 | DDC 736/.982—dc23
LC record available at https://lccn.loc.gov/2017000034

Manufactured in the United States by LSC Communications
81578102   2017
www.doverpublications.com

TABLE OF CONTENTS

SYMBOLS AND SIGNS

PROCEDURES

MISSILES

RAPIER

TALON

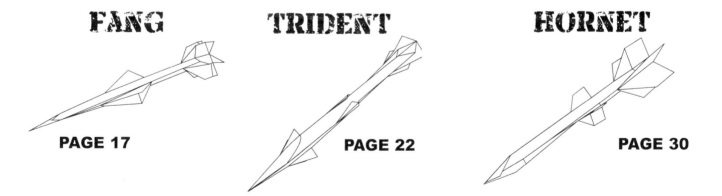

FANG

TRIDENT

HORNET

GROUND FORCES

HAVOC

LONGBOW

HELLSPAWN

NAVAL FORCES

POSEIDON

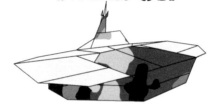

KRAKEN

TRITON

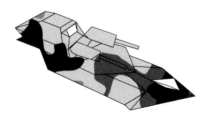

AIR FORCES

VANGUARD

PAGE 89

PHALANX

PAGE 95

VALKYRIE

PAGE 106

SABREWOLF

PAGE 117

SYMBOLS AND SIGNS

Lines

_____ This line indicates an edge.

·················· This line indicates a hidden edge.

- - - - - - - - - This line indicates where to make a valley fold.

- · - · - · - · - This lines indicates where to make a mountain fold.

··················· This lines indicates a hidden fold.

Arrows

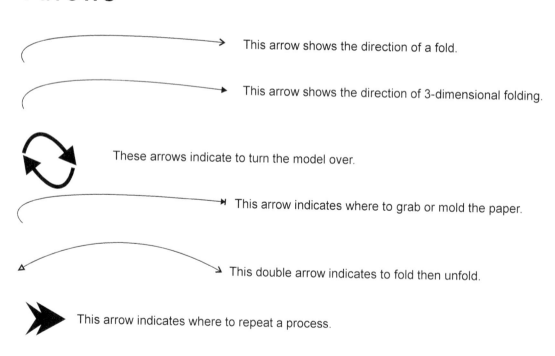

This arrow shows the direction of a fold.

This arrow shows the direction of 3-dimensional folding.

These arrows indicate to turn the model over.

This arrow indicates where to grab or mold the paper.

This double arrow indicates to fold then unfold.

This arrow indicates where to repeat a process.

PROCEDURES

Inside reverse fold

1.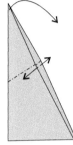

2.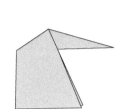

Partially open the sides out and push the top in.

Outside reverse fold

1.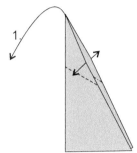

2.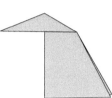

Partially open the sides out and push the top backward.

Squash fold

1.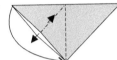

2.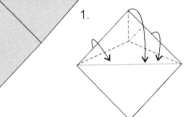

Pull the sides apart and push the corner down.

Rabbit ear fold

1.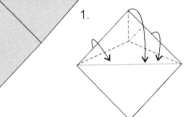

2.

3.

Push the two sides in and fold the corner over.

In progress.

Swivel fold

1.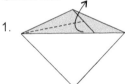

2.

3.

Pull the top layer up.

Continue to pull the layer until it lies flat. Push down the area that stands up.

Petal fold

1.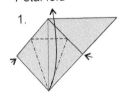

2.

3.

Pull the top layer up and push the sides in.

In progress.

Open sink

1.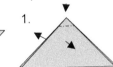

2.

3.

Push the top in and partially open the paper.

Continue to push the top and push the sides in.

Closed sink

1.

2.

3.

Push the top in while keeping the paper together.

In progress.

Preliminary fold

1.
2.
3.

Squash fold the flap down.

4.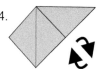

Turn the paper over.

5.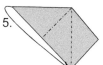

Squash fold the flap down.

6.

Jet fold

1.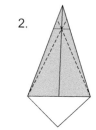
2.

Fold then unfold the sides as shown.

3.

Push the lower part in and push the sides together using the creases you just made.

4.

In progress.

5.

RAPIER MISSILE

Use a square measuring 2–6 inches.

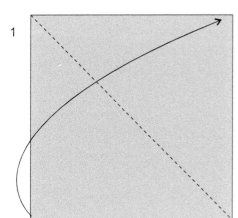

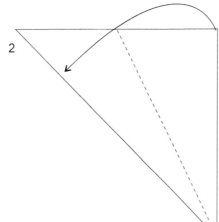

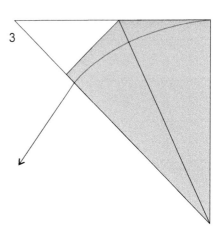

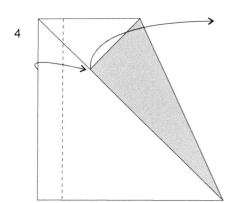

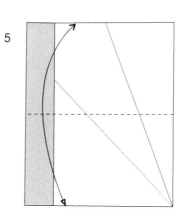

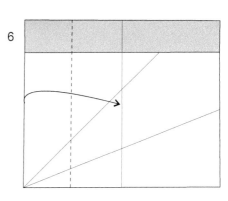

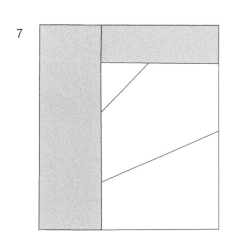

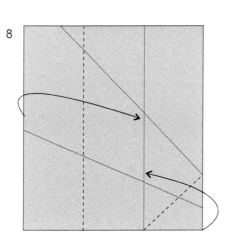

Turn the paper over.

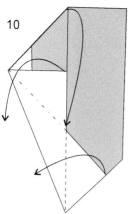

10

Simultaneously pull the trapped paper out and swivel fold it down. Then fold the bottom flap over.

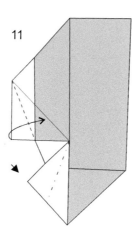

11

Fold the top flap over, then squash fold the bottom flap.

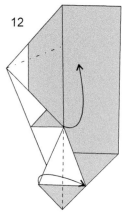

12

Swivel fold the top layer up, then fold the bottom flap over.

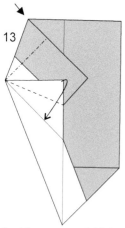

13

Inside reverse fold the top layer in, then valley fold the bottom layer down.

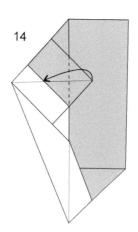

14

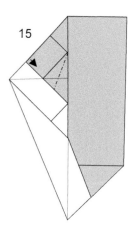

15

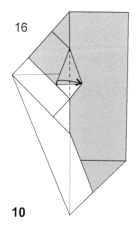

16

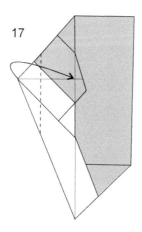

17

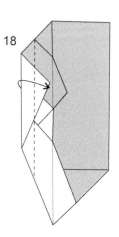

18

19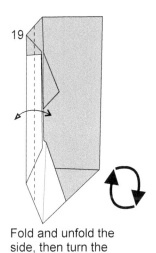

Fold and unfold the
side, then turn the
model over.

20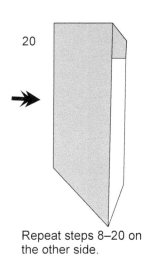

Repeat steps 8–20 on
the other side.

21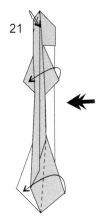

Narrow the
point, fold the
forward fin and
the tailfin over.
Then repeat to
the other side.

22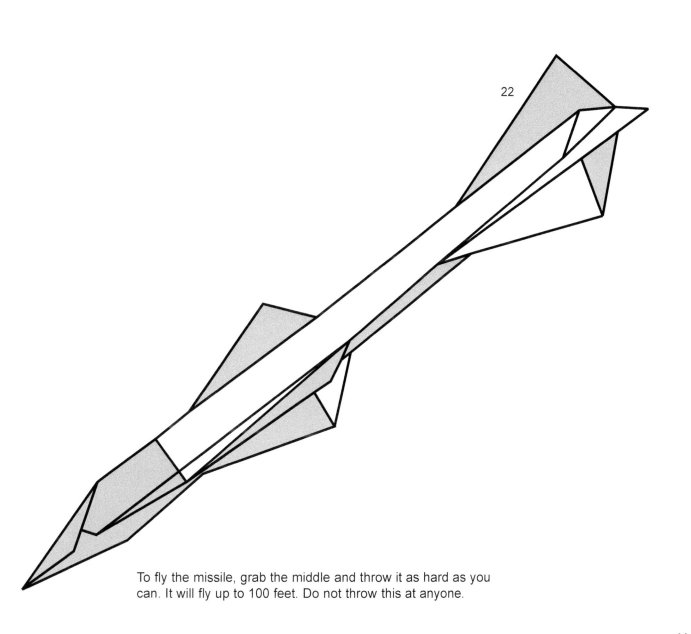

To fly the missile, grab the middle and throw it as hard as you
can. It will fly up to 100 feet. Do not throw this at anyone.

TALON MISSILE

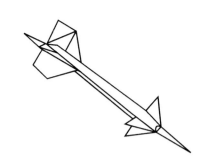

Use a 3–6-inch-square sheet of paper.

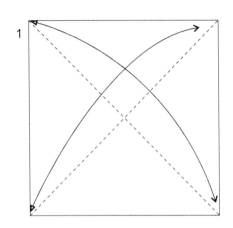

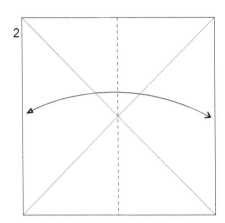

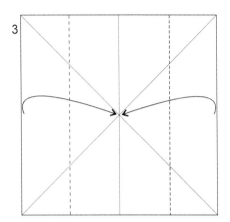

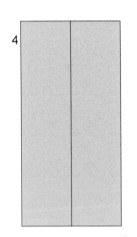

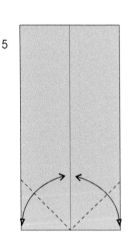

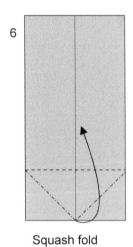

Squash fold
the bottom up.

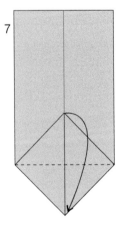

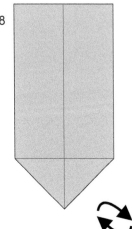

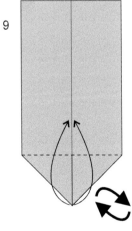

Fold the small flaps up,
then turn the model
over.

12

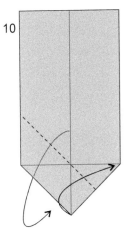

10

Simultaneously fold
the area over and
swing the small flap
from behind out.

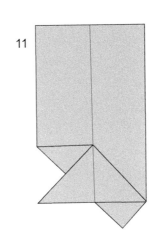

11

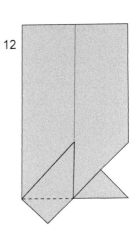

12

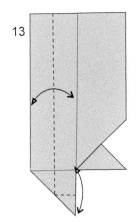

13

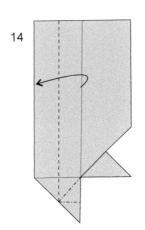

14

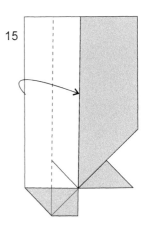

15

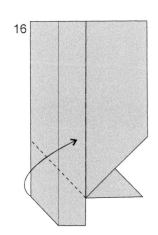

16

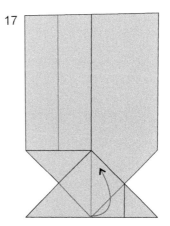

17

Fold the inner layer up. This
will free the paper that will
become a tailfin.

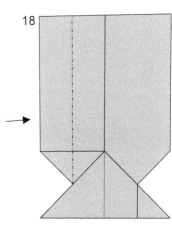

18

Closed sink the side of the
model in.

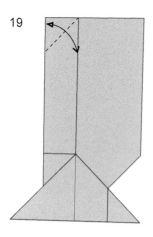

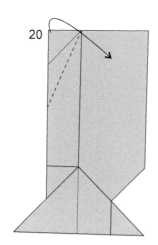

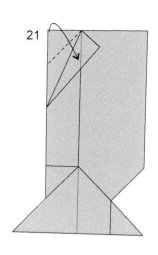

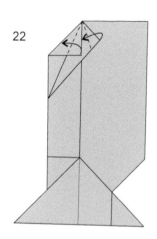

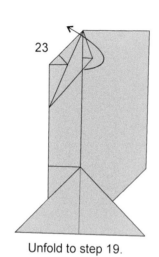

Unfold to step 19.

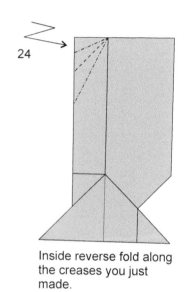

Inside reverse fold along the creases you just made.

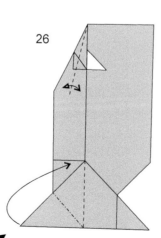

Swivel fold both layers of paper together.

14

Fold then unfold the top edge. Squash fold the bottom flap.

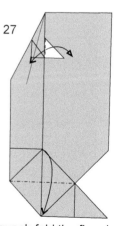

Squash fold the flap down. Fold then unfold both top flaps.

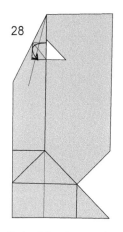

28

Swivel the trapped
paper down.

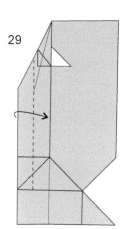

29

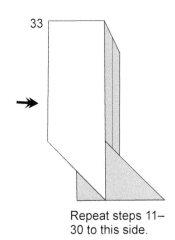

30

Fold then unfold the
side, then turn the
model over.

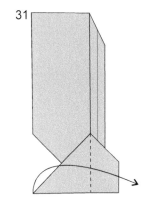

31

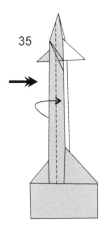

32

Wrap the layer from
behind around.

33

Repeat steps 11–
30 to this side.

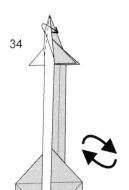

34

Fold the point in,
then turn the model
over.

35

Fold the side over, then
narrow the point as in
step 34.

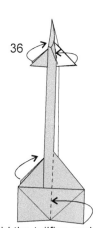

36

Fold the tailfins and
the canard fins
perpendicular to the
fuselage.

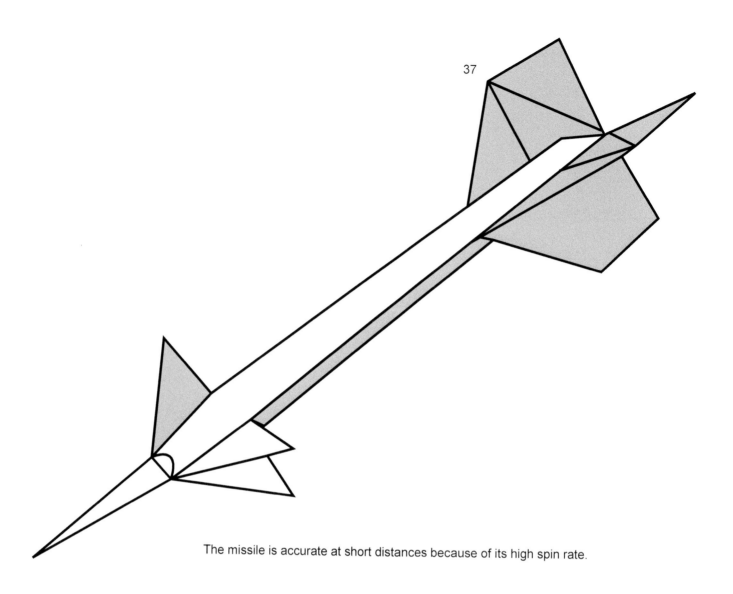

The missile is accurate at short distances because of its high spin rate.

FANG
GUIDED MUNITION

Use a square sheet of paper measuring at least 3 inches.

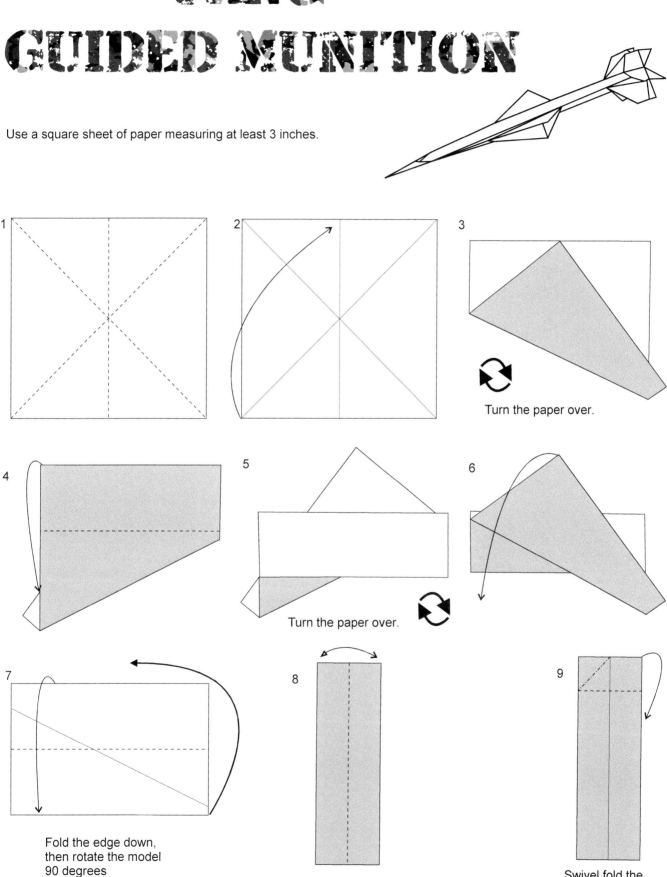

3 Turn the paper over.

5 Turn the paper over.

7 Fold the edge down, then rotate the model 90 degrees counterclockwise.

9 Swivel fold the paper down.

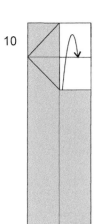

10

Inside reverse fold the paper under the layer behind it.

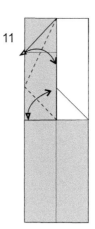

11

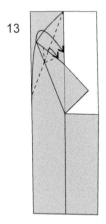

12

Using the bottom crease you made in step 11, partially fold the top layer over. The model will not lie flat.

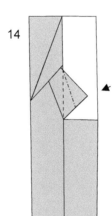

13

Fold the corner over while pushing the small inner area up.

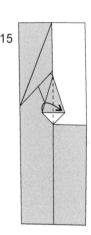

14

Squash fold the small flap over.

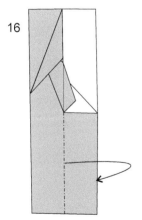

15

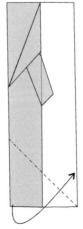

16

Mountain fold the top layer underneath the layer behind it.

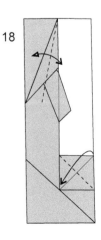

17

Inside reverse fold the corner over.

18

18

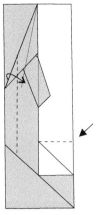

19

Fold the side over to the edge
shown. Inside reverse fold the small
flap at the bottom.

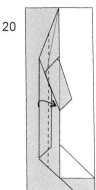

20

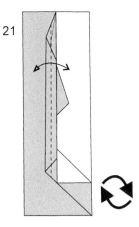

21

Fold and unfold the side
in half, then turn the
model over.

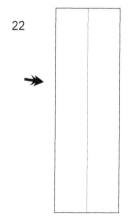

22

Repeat steps 8–16 to
this side.

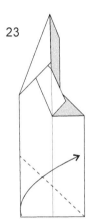

23

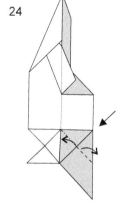

24

Pull apart the layers shown and
perform a modified squash fold.

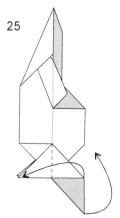

25

Swivel fold the flap
over and up.

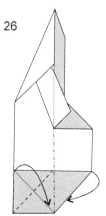

26

Fold the small corner down and
mountain fold the edge into the model.

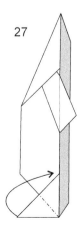

27

Squash fold the bottom
flap up.

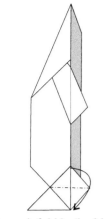

28

Squash fold both sides of the flap down.

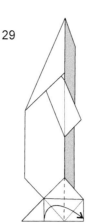

29

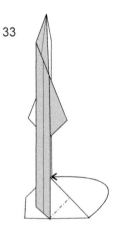

30

Repeat steps 27–29 to this flap.

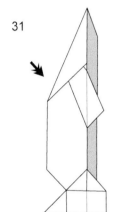

31

Repeat steps 18–21 to this side.

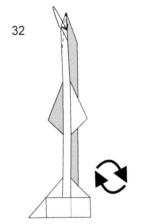

32

Narrow the point, then turn the model over.

33

Squash fold the flap over.

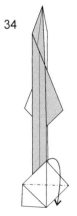

34

Squash fold both sides of the flap down.

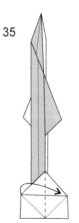

35

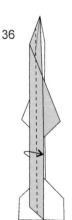

36

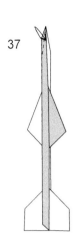

37

Narrow the point.

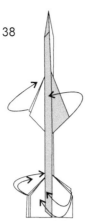

38

Fold the top canard fins perpendicular to each other. Then evenly space the six tailfins out.

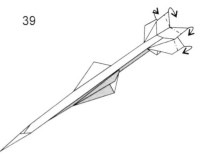

39

Slightly fold the six tailfins over in the same direction. Note this missile will not fly unless you do this.

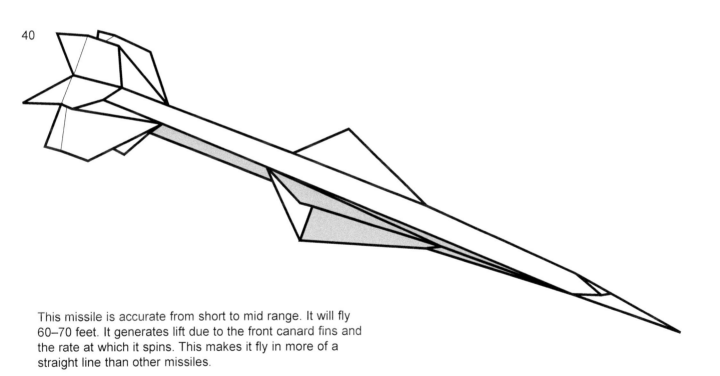

40

This missile is accurate from short to mid range. It will fly 60–70 feet. It generates lift due to the front canard fins and the rate at which it spins. This makes it fly in more of a straight line than other missiles.

TRIDENT MULTI ROLE MISSILE

Use a 3-inch-square sheet of thin paper.

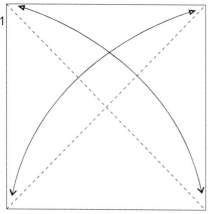

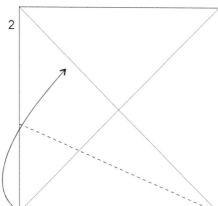

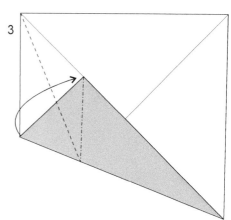

Rabbit ear fold the side in.

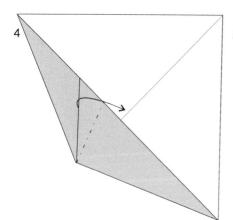

Inside reverse fold the flap in.

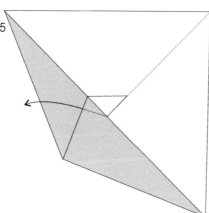

Pull the paper from underneath out.

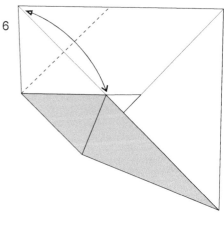

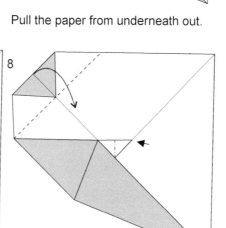

Fold the top down, then squash fold the small middle flap.

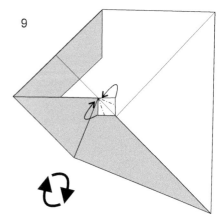

Mountain fold the sides of the small flap in, then turn the model over.

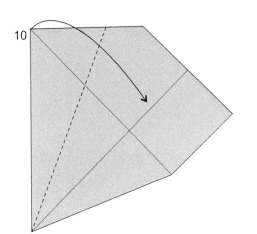

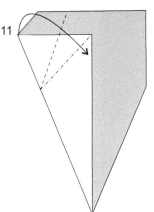

Rabbit ear fold the flap over.

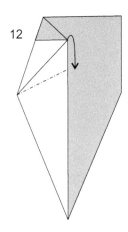

Inside reverse fold the flap down.

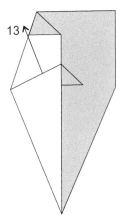

Pull the trapped paper up.

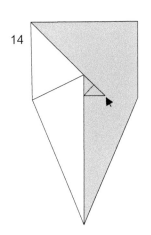

Squash fold the small flap.

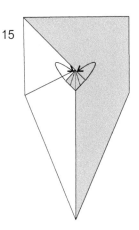

Fold the sides of the small flap in.

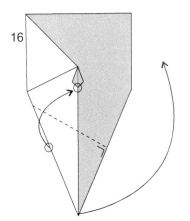

Fold the flap up perpendicular so that the areas shown meet.

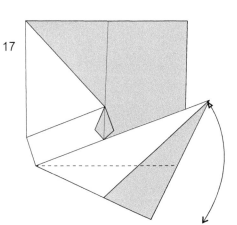

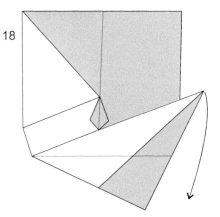

Fold the flap back to step 16.

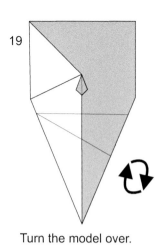

19

Turn the model over.

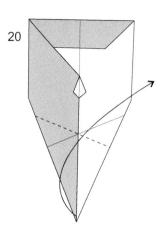

20

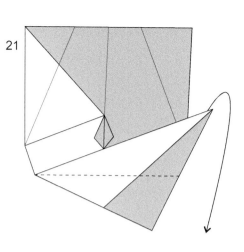

21

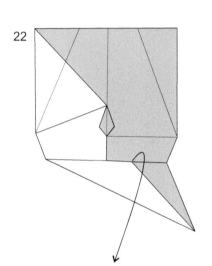

22

Return the model to step 19.

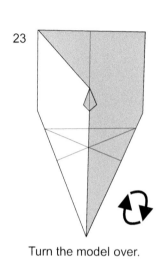

23

Turn the model over.

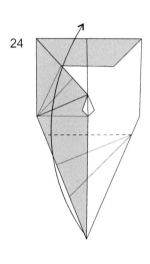

24

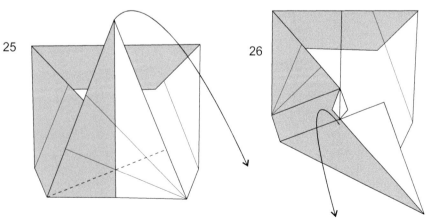

25

26

Pull the trapped paper from underneath out.

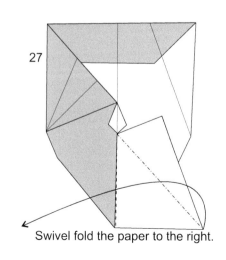

27

Swivel fold the paper to the right.

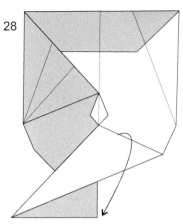

28 Pull the trapped paper from underneath out.

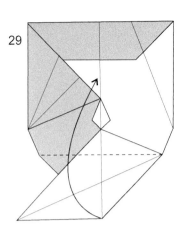

29

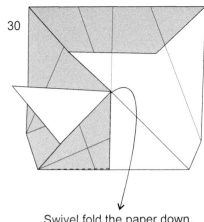

30 Swivel fold the paper down.

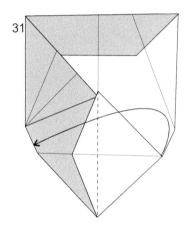

31

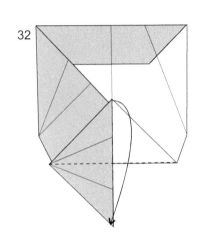

32

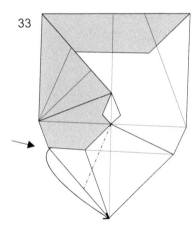

33 Squash fold the flap down.

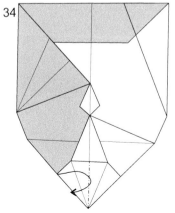

34 Inside reverse fold the flap behind.

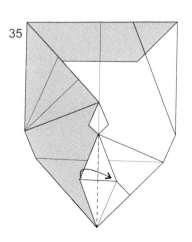

35

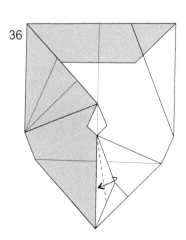

36

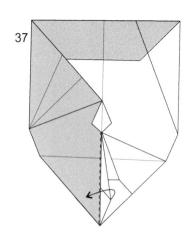

37

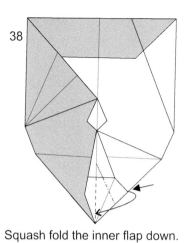

38

Squash fold the inner flap down.

39

Mountain fold the small layer behind.

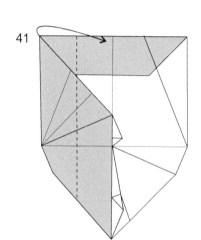

40

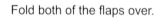

Fold both of the flaps over.

41

42

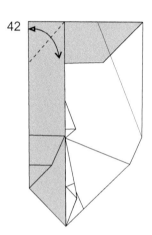

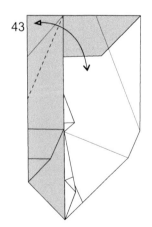

43

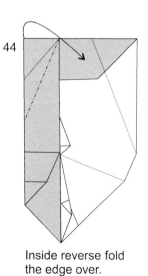

44

Inside reverse fold the edge over.

45

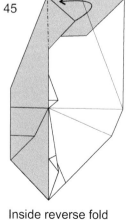

Inside reverse fold the edge over.

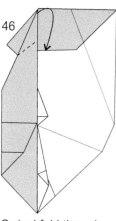

46

Swivel fold the edge down.

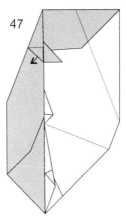

47

Pull the paper from underneath out.

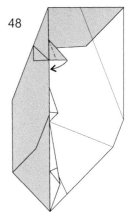

48

Inside reverse fold the flap down.

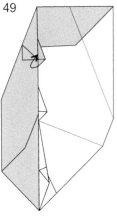

49

Mountain fold the small flap in.

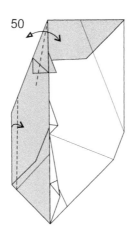

50

Fold then unfold the top point, then fold the side in using the flap behind as a guide.

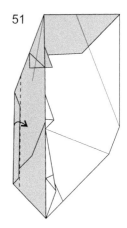

51

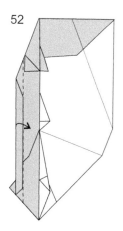

52

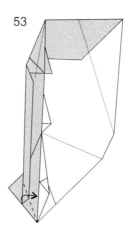

53

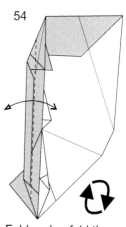

54

Fold and unfold the side over, then turn then model over.

27

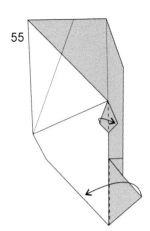

55

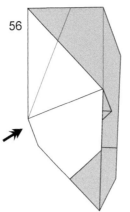

56

Repeat steps 41–51 to this side.

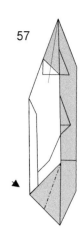

57

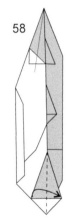

58

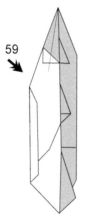

59

Repeat steps 51–53 to this side.

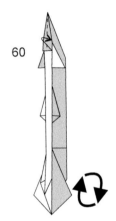

60

Narrow the point, then turn the model over.

61

62

Narrow the point. Fold both sets of fins perpendicular to each other. Fold the middle flaps over the fuselage. These will be used to attach to various vehicles.

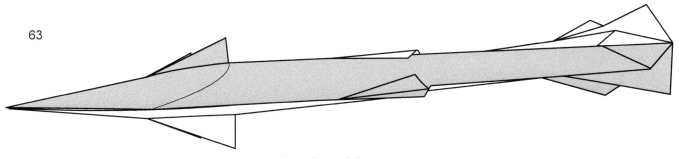

To fly this missile, grab the middle and give it a hard throw. It has
a range of up to 90 feet. Do not throw this directly at anyone.

HORNET GUIDED MUNITION

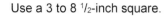

Use a 3 to 8 ½-inch square.

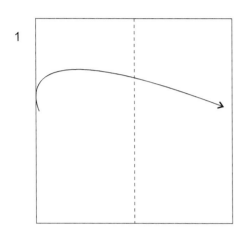

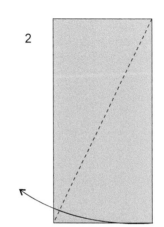

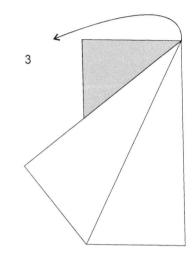

Using the corner behind, fold the edge over.

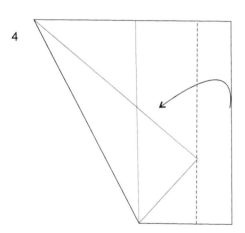

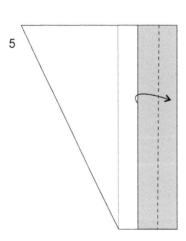

Slide the edge over to the center line.

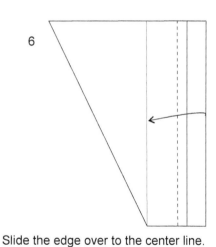

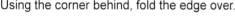

Fold the layer from behind out.

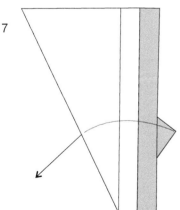

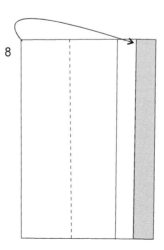

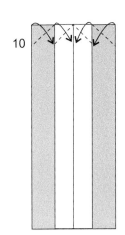

10

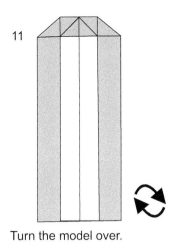

11

Turn the model over.

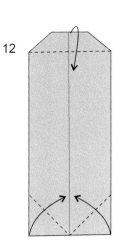

12

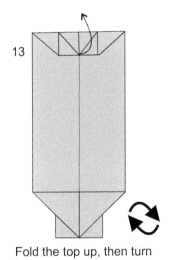

13

Fold the top up, then turn the model over.

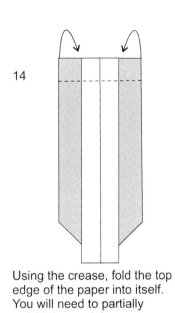

14

Using the crease, fold the top edge of the paper into itself. You will need to partially unfold the model.

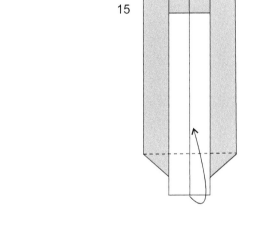

15

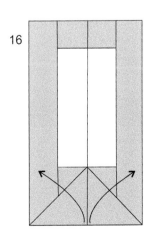

16

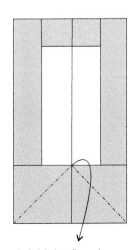

17

Squash fold the flap down.

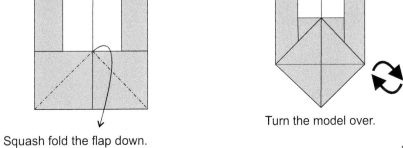

18

Turn the model over.

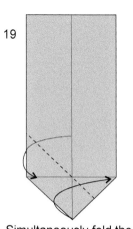

19

Simultaneously fold the corner over and swing the flap from behind around.

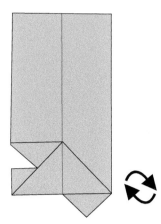

20

Turn the model over.

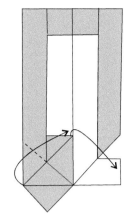

21

Swivel the bottom flap over.

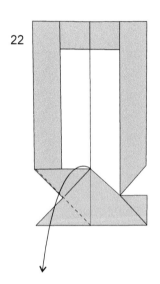

22

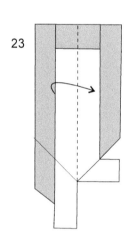

23

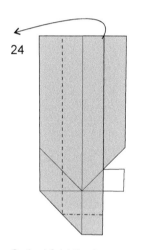

24

Swivel fold the layer over.

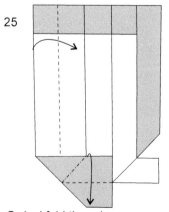

25

Swivel fold the edge over as shown.

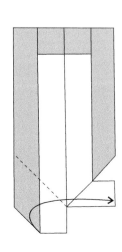

26

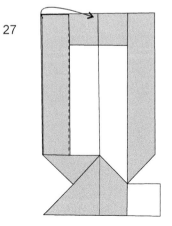

27

Fold the top layer only over.

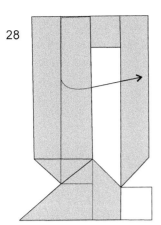

28

Pull out the inner layer. Use step 29 as a reference.

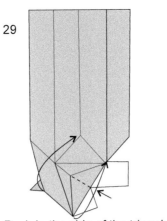

29

Push in the side of the triangle that forms, and reform the model.

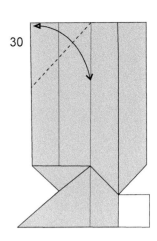

30

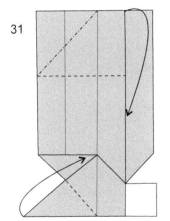

31

Squash fold the top using the crease you just made, then squash fold the bottom flap.

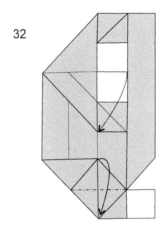

32

Inside reverse fold the inner layer of paper down, then squash fold the small flap out.

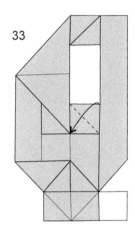

33

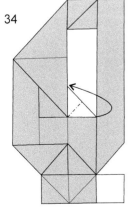

34

Squash fold the flap up.

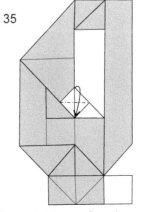

35

Squash fold the flap down.

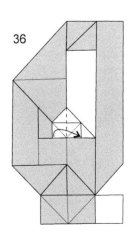

36

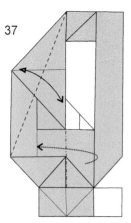

37

Fold and unfold the top
edge, then mountain fold
the inner excess layer in.

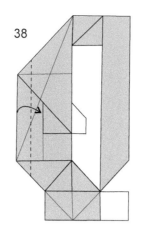

38

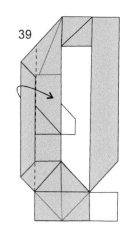

39

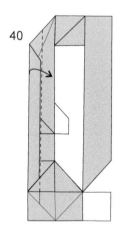

40

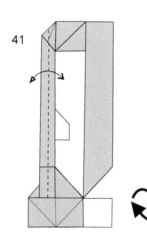

41

Fold then unfold the side. Turn
the model over.

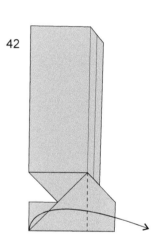

42

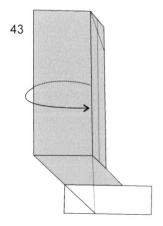

43

Wrap the layer behind around
the edge.

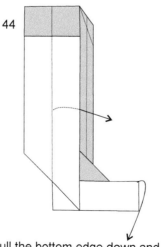

44

Pull the bottom edge down and
swing the inner edge out.

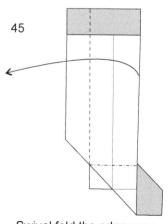

45

Swivel fold the edge over.

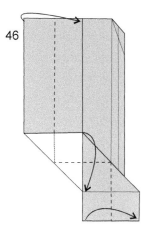

46

Perform a double swivel
fold to the top layer.

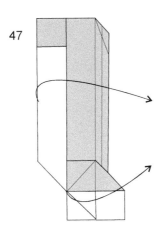

47

Unfold the top part of the model
to step 45. Leave the flaps
folded.

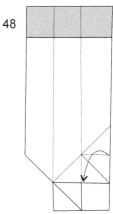

48

Inside reverse fold
the small inner area.

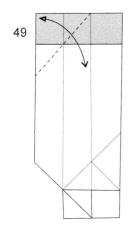

49

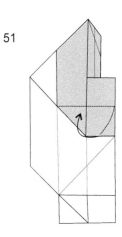

50

Swivel fold the flap down.

51

Wrap the paper from
underneath around.

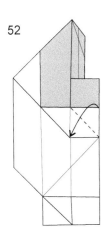

52

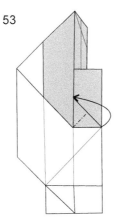

53

Squash fold the
flap up.

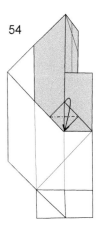

54

Squash fold the
flap down.

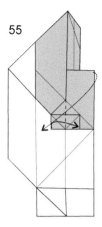

55

Fold the small flap over, then inside reverse fold the inside area.

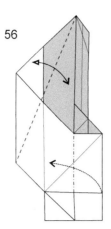

56

Fold then unfold the edge, then mountain fold the inner edge in.

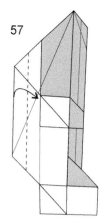

57

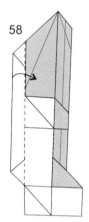

58

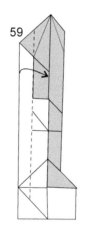

59

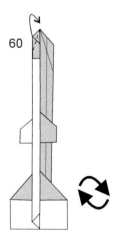

60

Narrow the point, then turn the model over.

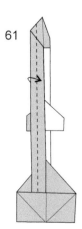

61

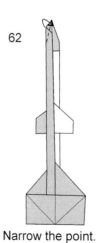

62

Narrow the point.

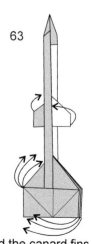

63

Fold the canard fins perpendicular to each other, then evenly space out the tailfins.

64

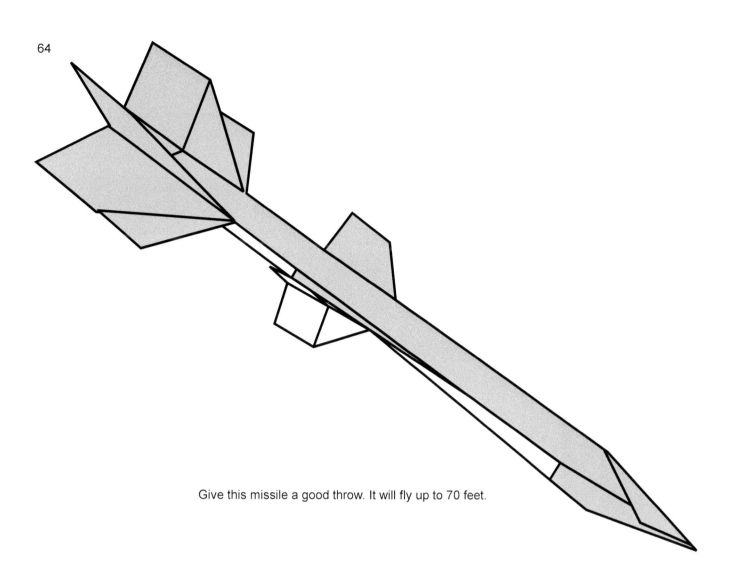

Give this missile a good throw. It will fly up to 70 feet.

HAVOC ASSAULT RIFLE

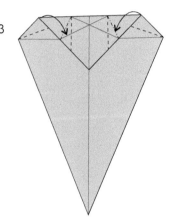

Use a square sheet of paper of a size that suits your needs.

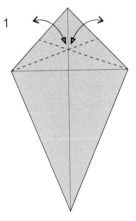

1

Begin with a bird base. Fold and unfold the top triangle.

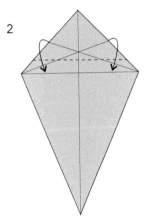

2

Fold the top down using the creases you just made.

3

Swivel fold the edges in.

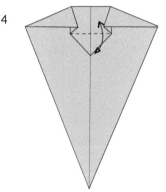

4

Fold then unfold the area shown.

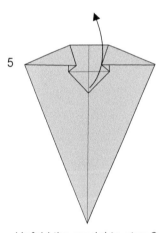

5

Unfold the model to step 2.

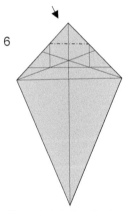

6

Closed sink the tip down.

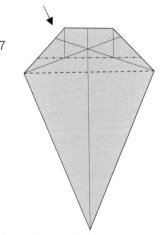

7

Spread squash the area down using the creases made.

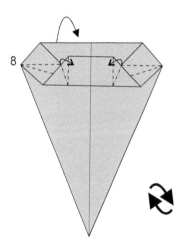

8

Swivel fold the edges. Then fold the paper behind down and turn the model over.

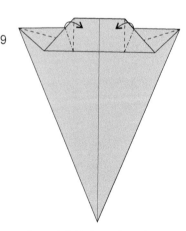

9

Swivel fold the edges in.

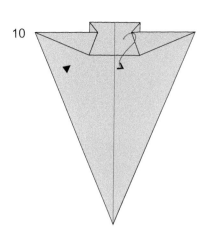

10

Closed sink the area into the layer just underneath it. Repeat behind.

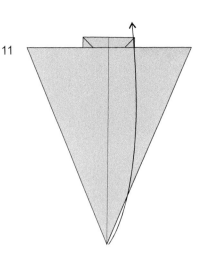

11

Fold one flap up.

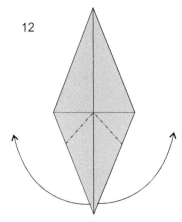

12

Squash fold the points down.

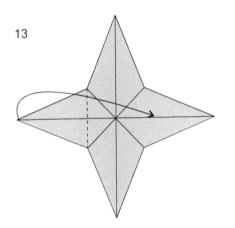

13

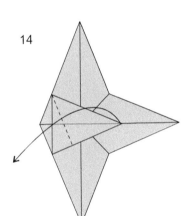

14

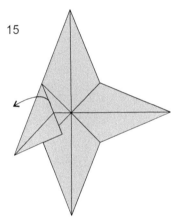

15

Pull the trapped paper from underneath out.

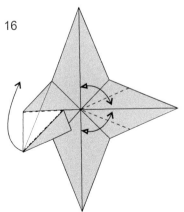

16

Fold then unfold the inner edges of the flap shown. Swivel fold the flap shown over.

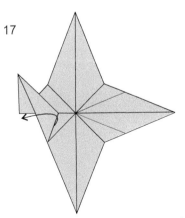

17

Pull the trapped paper from underneath out.

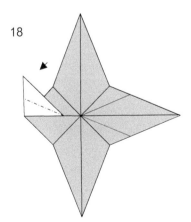

18

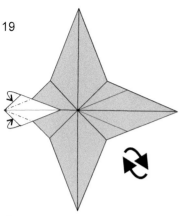

19

Petal fold the flap and turn the model over.

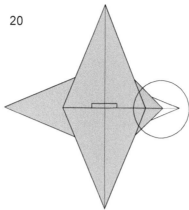

20

The next few steps will focus on the area circled.

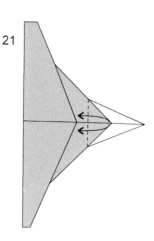

21

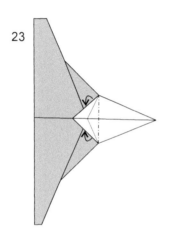

22

Fold then unfold the small flaps.

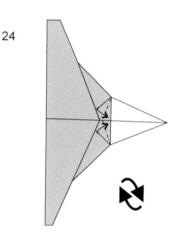

23

Outside wrap the small flaps into the model.

24

Outside reverse fold the small flaps down, then turn the model over.

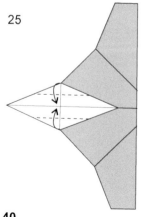

25

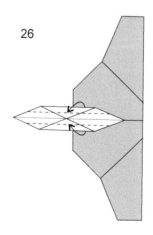

26

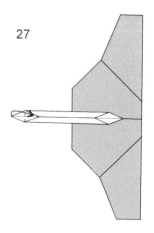

27

28

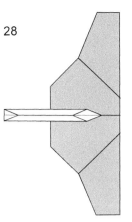

The remaining steps will focus back on the rest of the model.

29

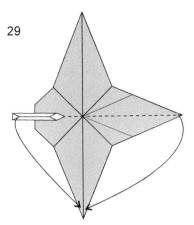

Fold the flaps back down.

30

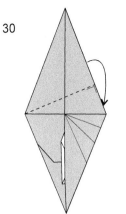

Fold the flap down perpendicular to itself.

31

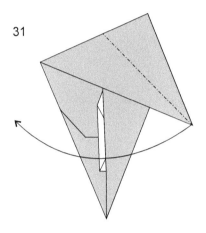

Swivel the flap over.

32

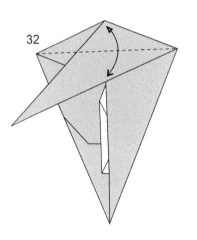

33

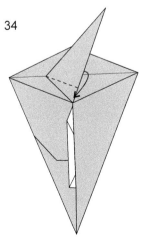

Fold the flap up perpendicular to itself.

34

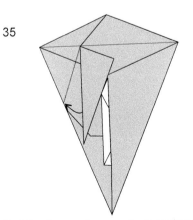

Fold the flap down perpendicular to itself.

35

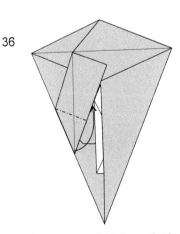

Pull the trapped paper from underneath out.

36

Inside reverse fold the point in.

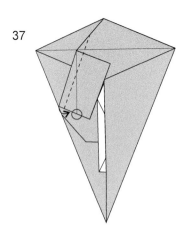

37

Fold the side over about 1/3 the
way to the line shown.

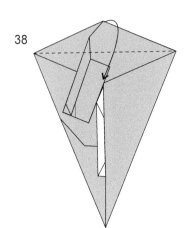

38

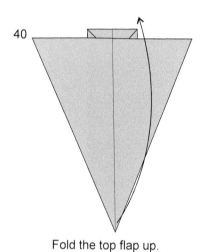

Turn the model over.

39

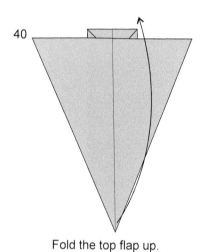

40

Fold the top flap up.

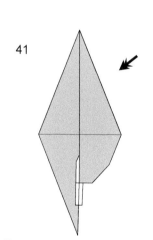

41

Repeat steps 31–32 to this
flap.

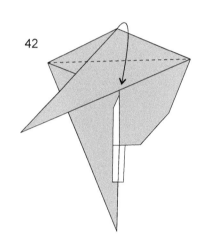

42

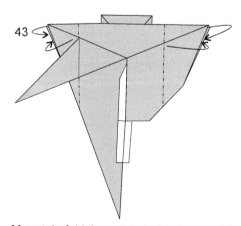

43

Mountain fold the points inside the model.

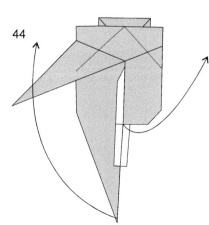

44

Inside reverse fold the flaps up.

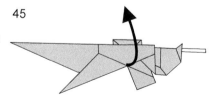

45

Open the model so the middle is
exposed.

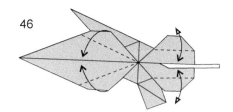

46

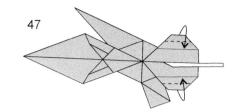

47

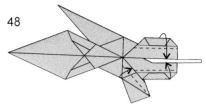

48

Fold the sides of the flap in. Fold the small corner over.

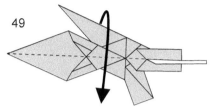

49

Fold the model in half.

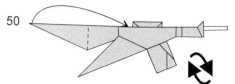

50

Fold the flap in then turn the model over.

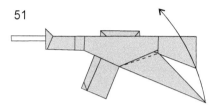

51

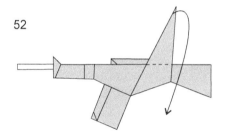

52

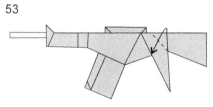

53

54

Slide some paper from underneath over.

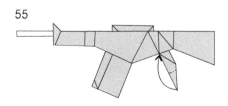

55

Inside reverse fold the small point in.

56

Move the small area into the model.

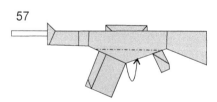

57

Mountain fold the small section into the model, then turn the model over.

58

Mountain fold the small section into the model.

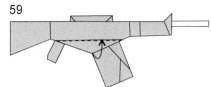

59

Valley fold the small section into the model.

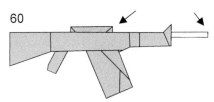

60

Round the barrel and the sight.

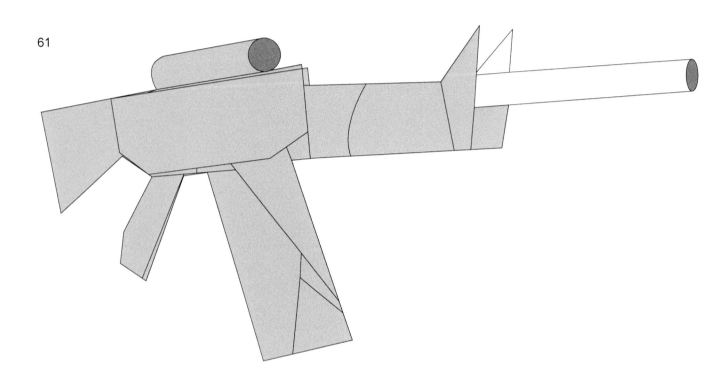

61

LONGBOW SNIPER RIFLE

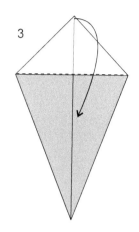

Use a square sheet of paper of a size that suits your needs.

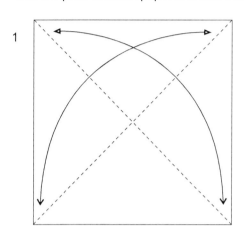

1

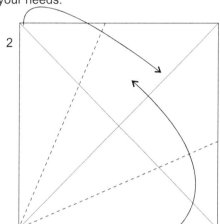

2

3

4

5

Squash fold the top,
repeat behind.

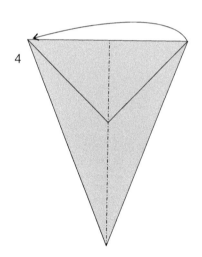

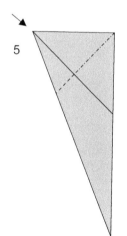

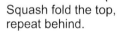

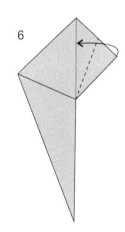

6

7

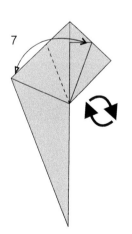

Turn the model over.

8

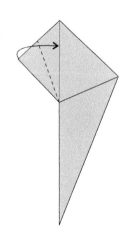

9

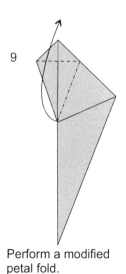

Perform a modified
petal fold.

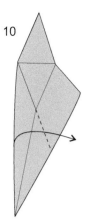

10

Step 9 in
progress.
Continue to fold
the flap over
and lay it flat.

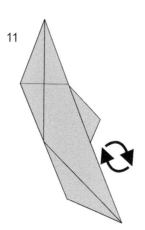

11

Turn the model over.

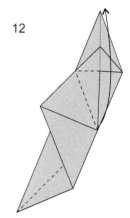

12

Perform a modified
petal fold.

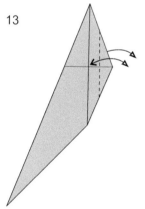

13

Fold then unfold the
sides in, repeat behind.

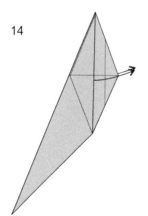

14

Pull the trapped paper from
underneath out. Repeat
behind.

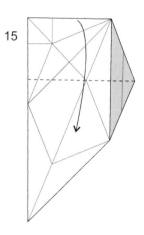

15

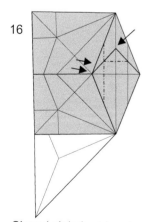

16

Closed sink the triangle
in. Open sink the sides of
the bird base in.

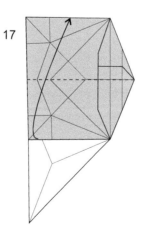

17

Fold the flap over. Repeat
behind.

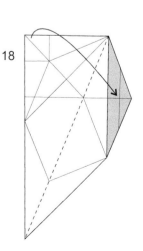

18

19

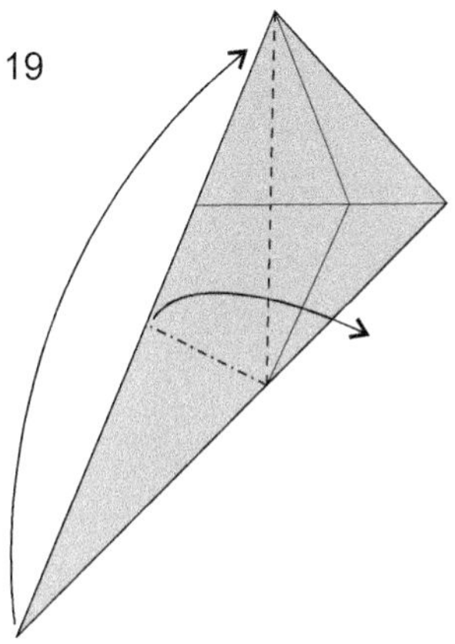

Open the flap up and fold it flat.

20

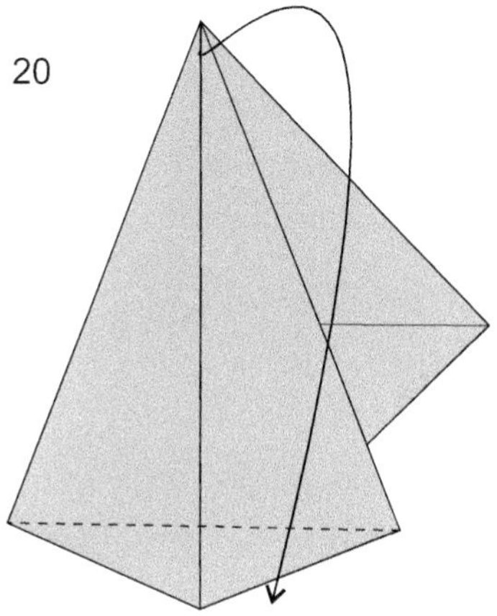

21

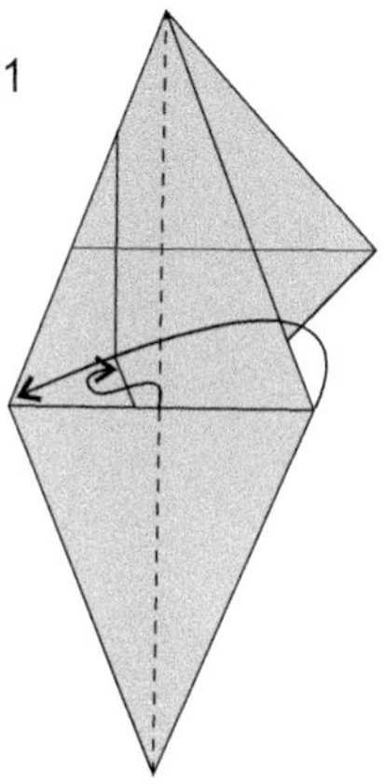

Simultaneously tuck the area indicated into the model and fold the flap in half.

22

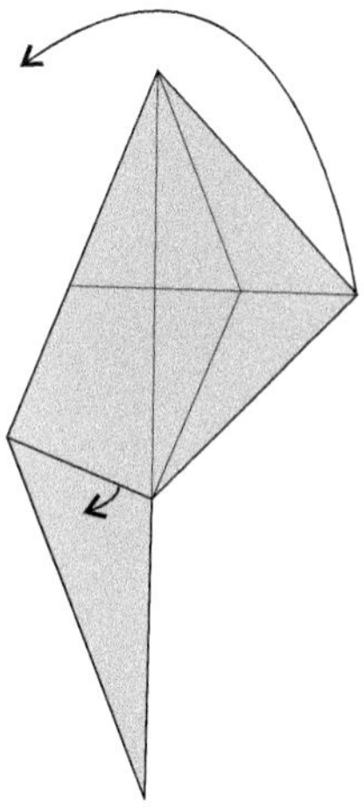

Simultaneously pull the trapped paper out and swing the layer over.

23

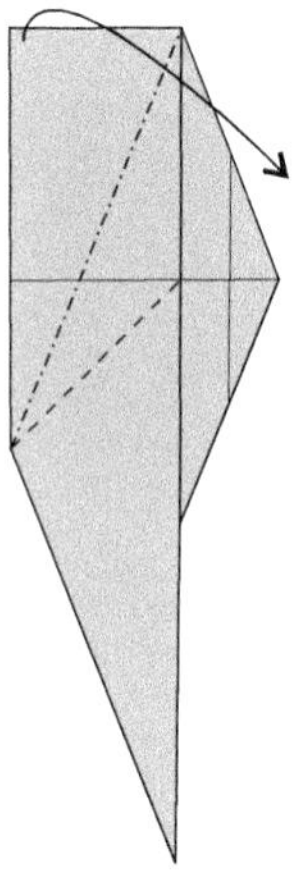

Swivel fold the flap over.

24

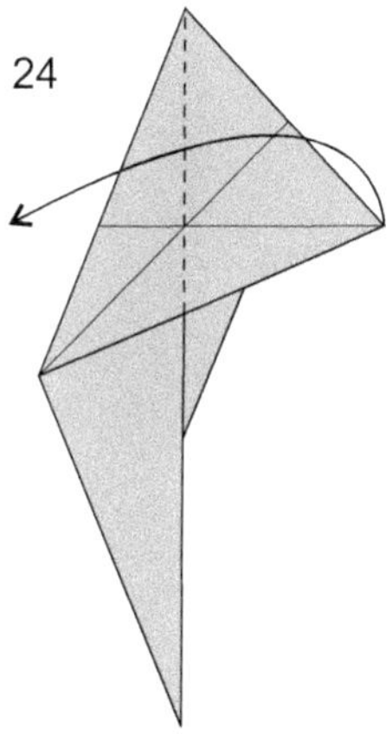

25

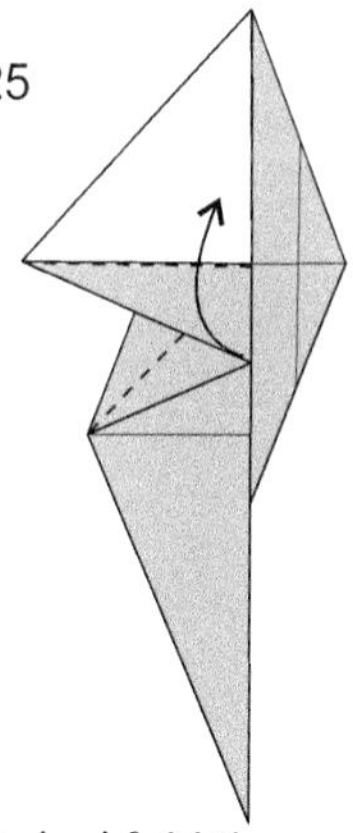

Swivel fold the paper up.

26

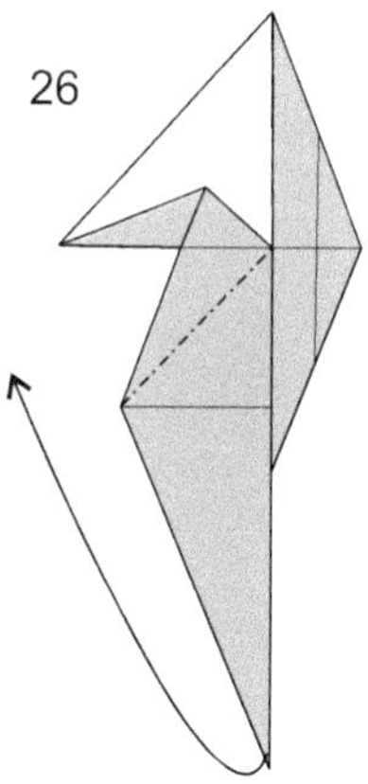

Squash fold the flap up.

27

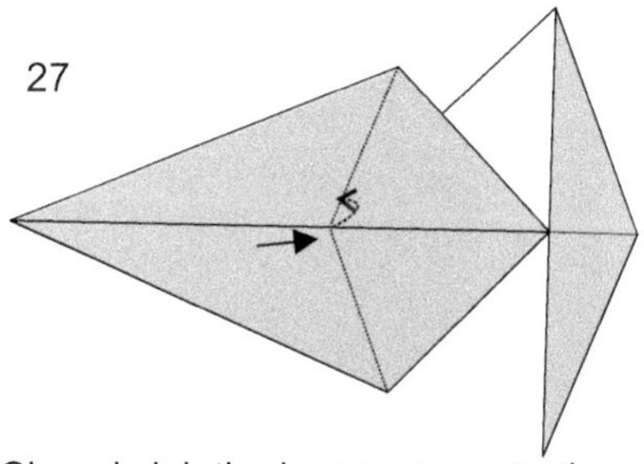

Closed sink the inner area onto the layer behind it.

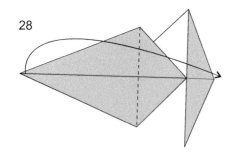

28

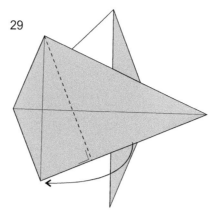

29

Fold the flap over perpendicular as shown.

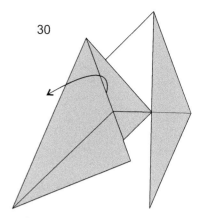

30

Pull the trapped paper out.

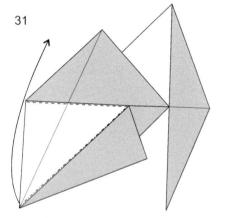

31

Swivel fold the flap over.

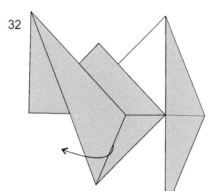

32

Pull the trapped paper out.

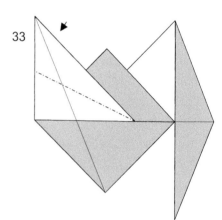

33

Squash fold the flap.

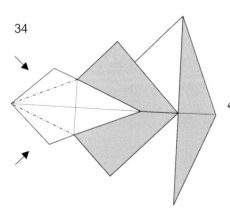

34

Reverse fold the edges in.

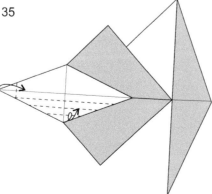

35

Fold the side into fourths and fold it up. Then fold the tip in.

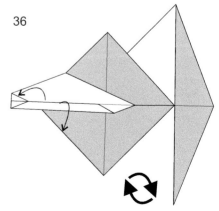

36

Return the model to step 35, then turn the model over.

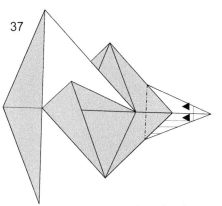

37

Inside reverse fold the flaps in, then turn the model over.

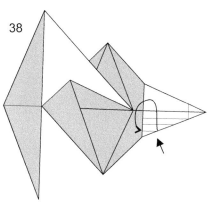

38

Closed wrap the bottom edge around.

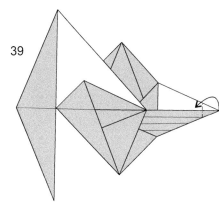

39

Inside reverse fold the tip in.

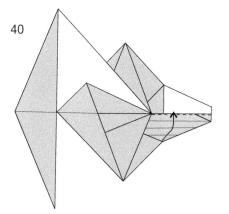

40

Valley fold the bottom into the top.

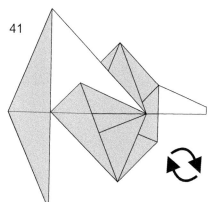

41

Turn the model over.

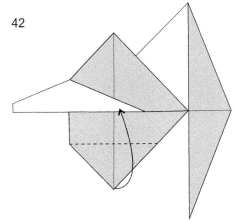

42

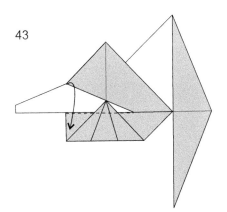

43

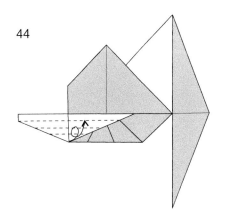

44

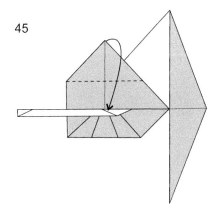

45

46

47

48

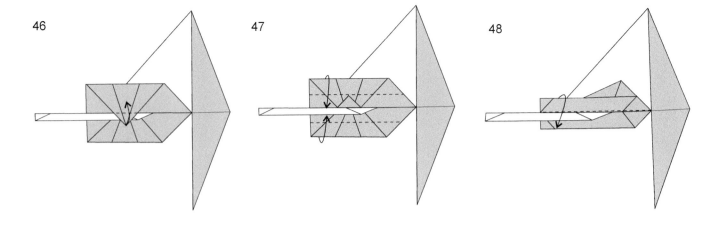

49

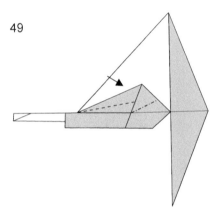

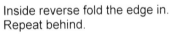

Inside reverse fold the edge in.
Repeat behind.

50

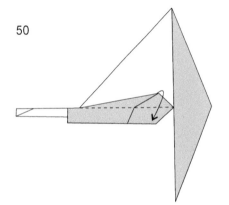

Valley fold the flap down. Repeat behind.

51

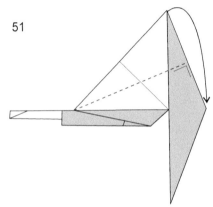

Fold the flap down perpendicular to
itself. Repeat behind.

52

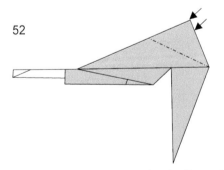

Inside reverse fold the edge in. Repeat
behind.

53

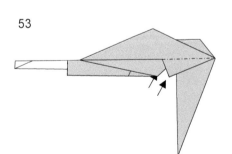

Inside reverse fold the edge in. Repeat
behind.

54

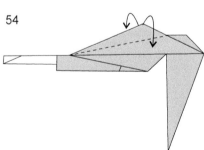

Valley fold the side down. Repeat
behind.

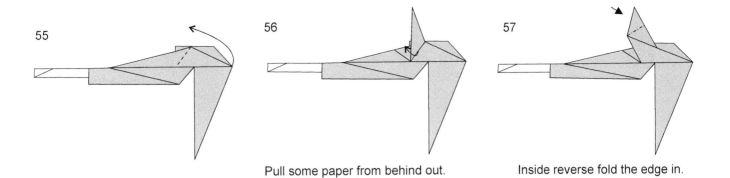

55

56

Pull some paper from behind out.

57

Inside reverse fold the edge in.

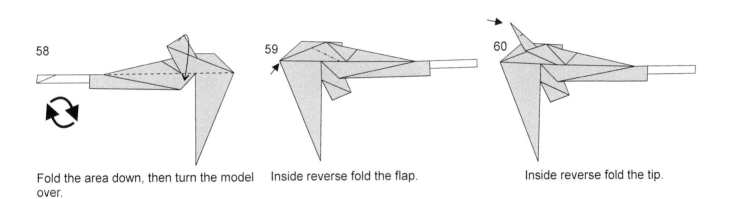

58

Fold the area down, then turn the model over.

59

Inside reverse fold the flap.

60

Inside reverse fold the tip.

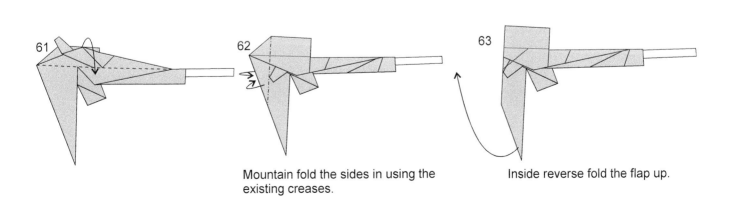

61

62

Mountain fold the sides in using the existing creases.

63

Inside reverse fold the flap up.

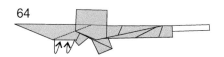

64

Mountain fold the sides in.

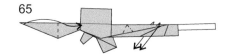

65

Valley fold the stock in and crimp the legs down.

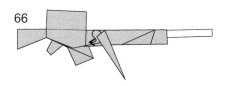

66

Tuck the corner of the legs into the pocket behind.

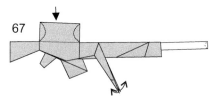

67

Round the scope, round the barrel, and fold the feet out.

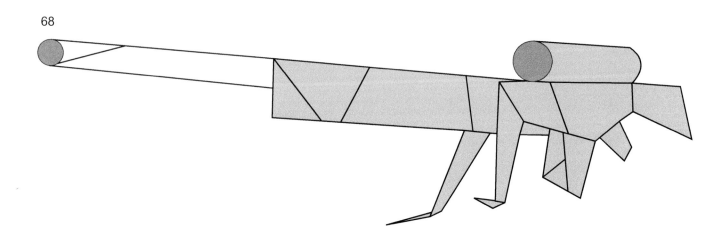

68

HELLSPAWN ASSAULT INFANTRY

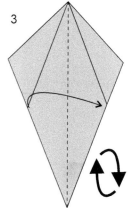

Use a square sheet of foil paper to suit your needs.

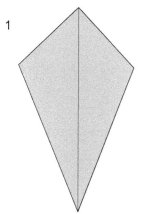

1

Begin with a bird base.

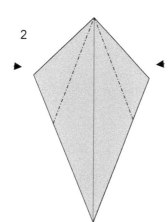

2

Sink the sides in.

3

Fold one layer over, then turn the model over.

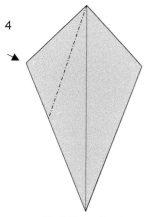

4

Sink the edge in.

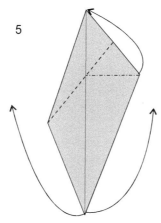

5

Swivel fold the flaps out and fold the small triangular area up.

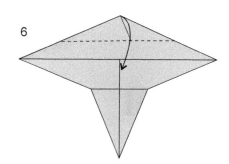

6

Fold the area down as shown and petal fold the small flap behind.

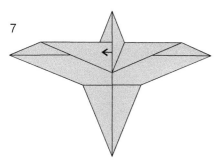

7

Pull the trapped paper from underneath out.

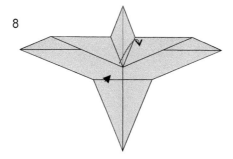

8

Closed sink the area behind the layer it is directly on top of.

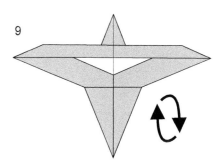

9

Turn the model over.

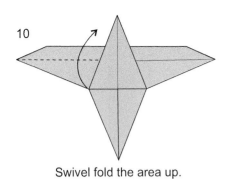

10

Swivel fold the area up.

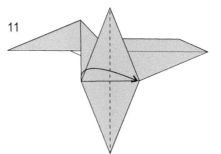

11

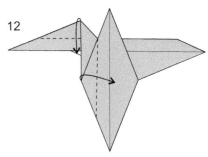

12

Swivel fold the edge over as shown.

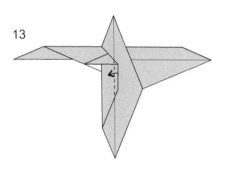

13

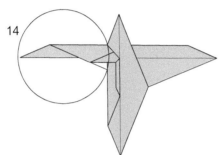

14

The next series of steps will focus on the area circled.

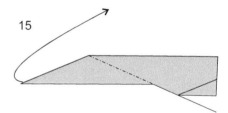

15

Inside reverse fold the flap up.

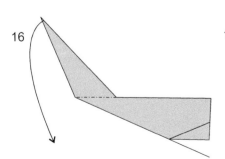

16

Inside reverse fold the flap down.

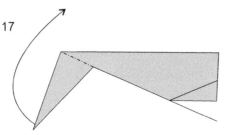

17

Inside reverse fold the flap up.

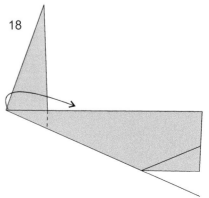

18

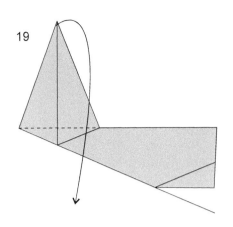

19

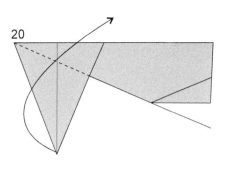

20

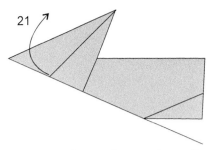

21

Pull the trapped paper from underneath up.

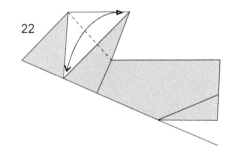

22

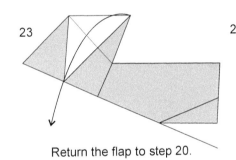

23

Return the flap to step 20.

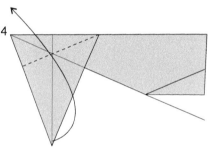

24

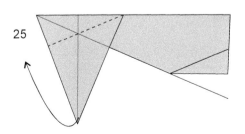

25

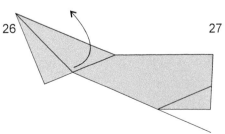

26

Pull the trapped paper from underneath up.

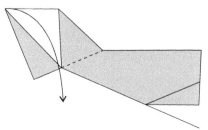

27

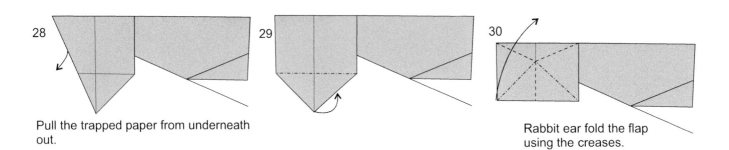

28 Pull the trapped paper from underneath out.

29

30 Rabbit ear fold the flap using the creases.

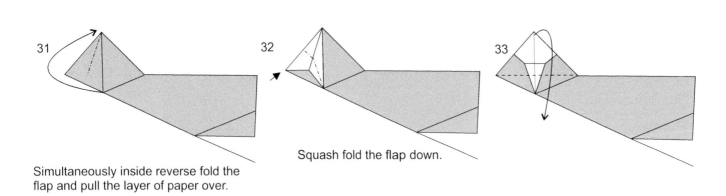

31 Simultaneously inside reverse fold the flap and pull the layer of paper over.

32 Squash fold the flap down.

33

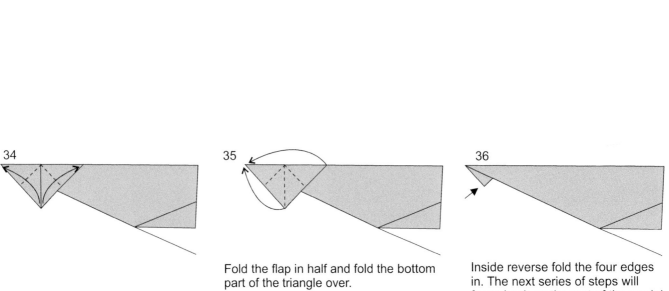

34

35 Fold the flap in half and fold the bottom part of the triangle over.

36 Inside reverse fold the four edges in. The next series of steps will focus back on the rest of the model.

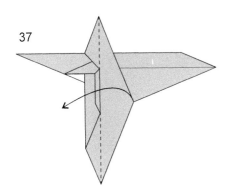

37

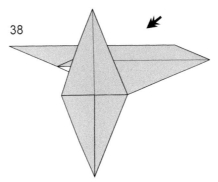

38

Repeat steps 14–37 to this side.

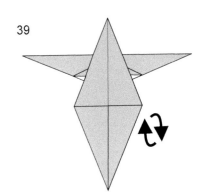

39

Turn the model over.

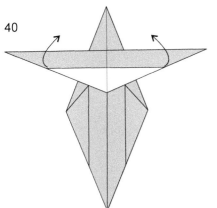

40

Pull the layer of paper upward.

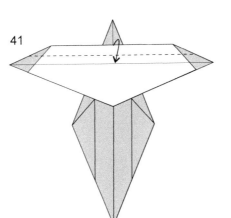

41

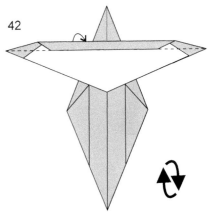

42

Fold the edge into the pocket behind,
then turn the model over.

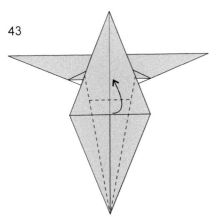

43

Perform a modified petal fold.

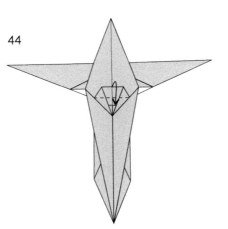

44

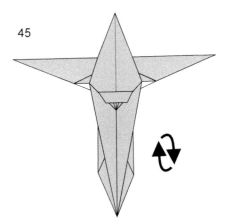

45

Turn the model over.

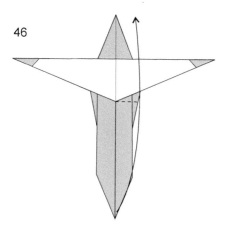

46

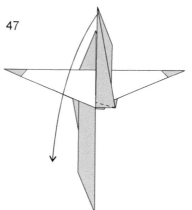

47

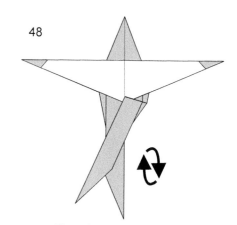

48

Turn the model over.

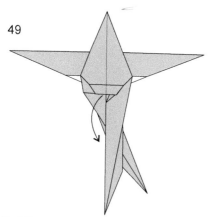

49

Pull the trapped paper from underneath out.

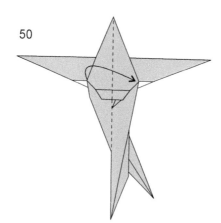

50

Open the side of the model. It will not lie flat.

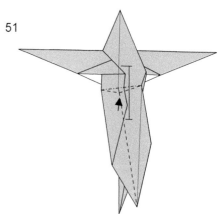

51

Using the creases, crimp the area into the model. Make sure that the layer shown stays to the right.

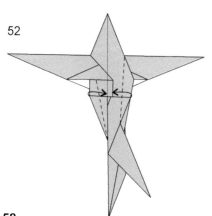

52

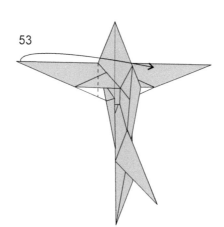

53

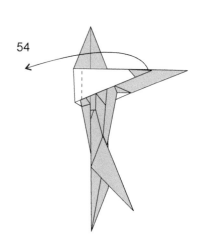

54

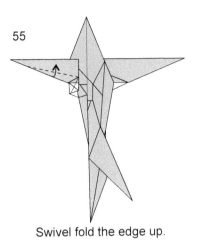

55

Swivel fold the edge up.

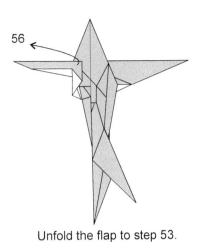

56

Unfold the flap to step 53.

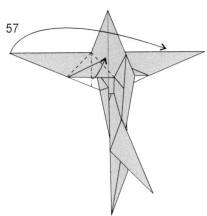

57

Fold the flap back while folding the center up.

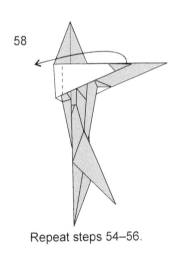

58

Repeat steps 54–56.

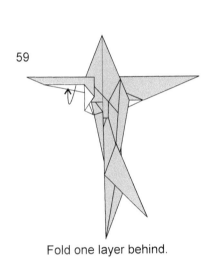

59

Fold one layer behind.

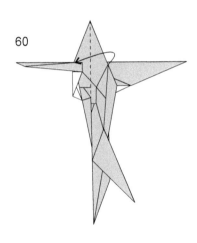

60

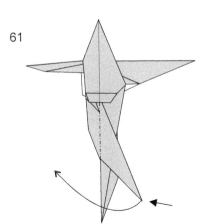

61

Inside reverse fold the flap over.

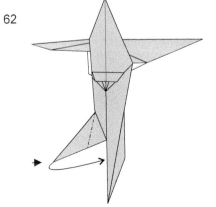

62

Squash fold the flap as shown. The next set of steps can be folded to your liking.

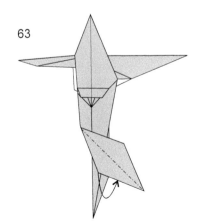

63

64

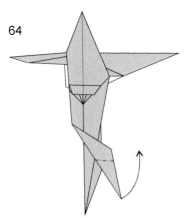

Inside reverse fold the flap up.

65

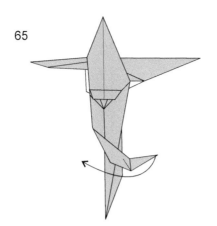

Inside reverse fold the flap.

66

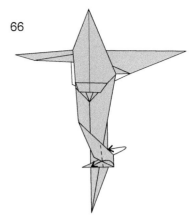

Swivel fold the foot in the front and back.

67

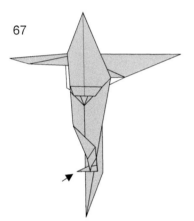

Inside reverse fold the tip in.

68

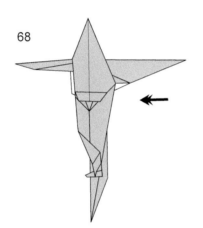

Repeat steps 46–68 to this side.

69

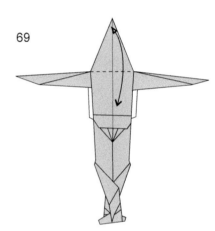

70

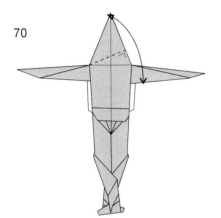

Fold then unfold the flap perpendicular to itself.

71

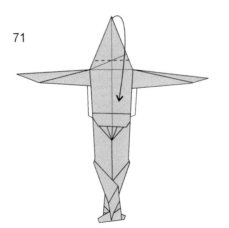

72

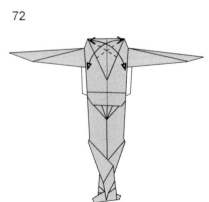

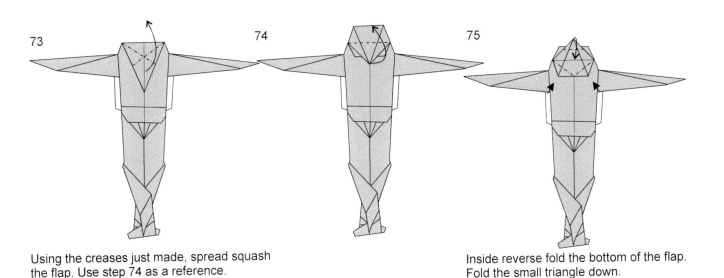

73

Using the creases just made, spread squash the flap. Use step 74 as a reference.

74

75

Inside reverse fold the bottom of the flap. Fold the small triangle down.

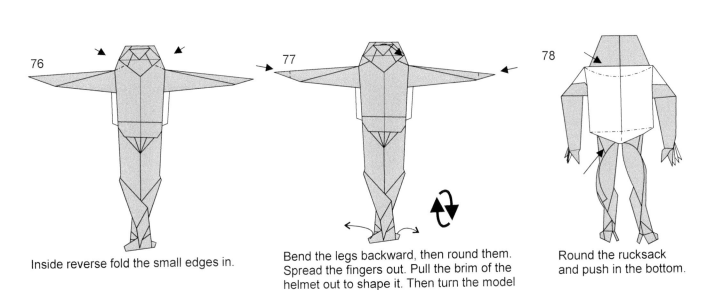

76

Inside reverse fold the small edges in.

77

Bend the legs backward, then round them. Spread the fingers out. Pull the brim of the helmet out to shape it. Then turn the model over.

78

Round the rucksack and push in the bottom.

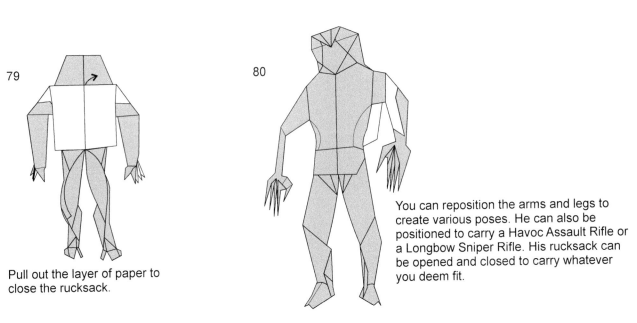

79

Pull out the layer of paper to close the rucksack.

80

You can reposition the arms and legs to create various poses. He can also be positioned to carry a Havoc Assault Rifle or a Longbow Sniper Rifle. His rucksack can be opened and closed to carry whatever you deem fit.

POSEIDON AIRCRAFT CARRIER

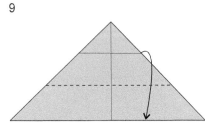

Use a square sheet of paper as large as you can acquire.

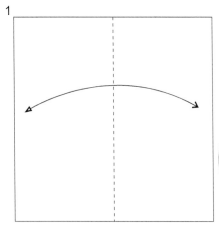

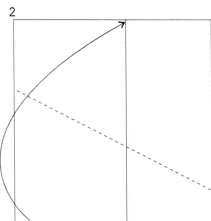

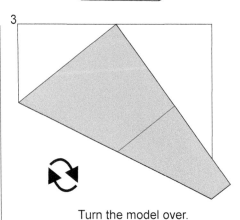

Turn the model over.

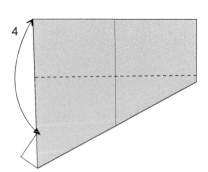

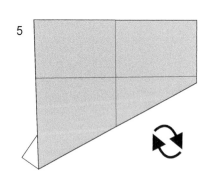

Turn the model over.

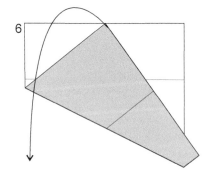

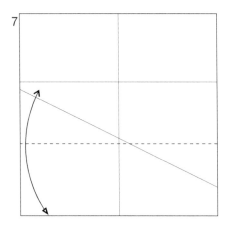

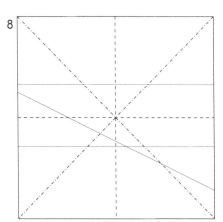

Form a waterbomb base.

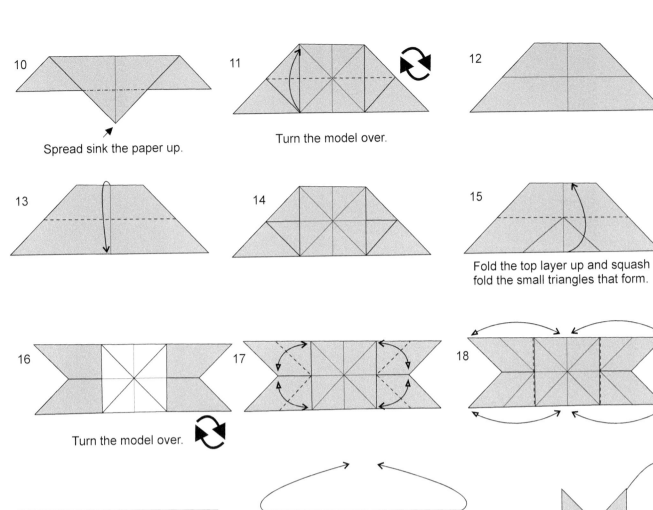

10

Spread sink the paper up.

11

Turn the model over.

12

13

14

15

Fold the top layer up and squash fold the small triangles that form.

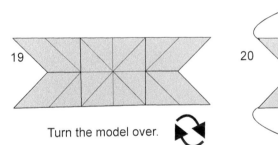

16

Turn the model over.

17

18

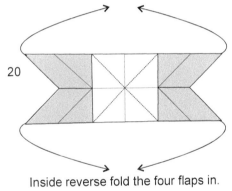

19

Turn the model over.

20

Inside reverse fold the four flaps in.

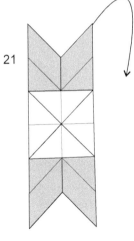

21

Fold the flap so it stands upright.

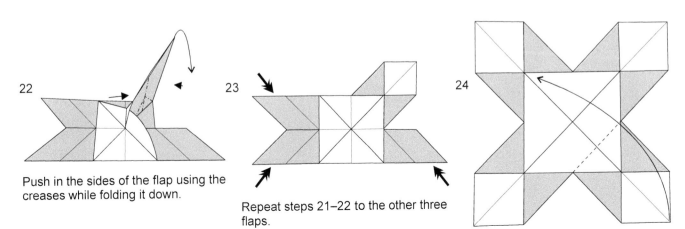

22

Push in the sides of the flap using the creases while folding it down.

23

Repeat steps 21–22 to the other three flaps.

24

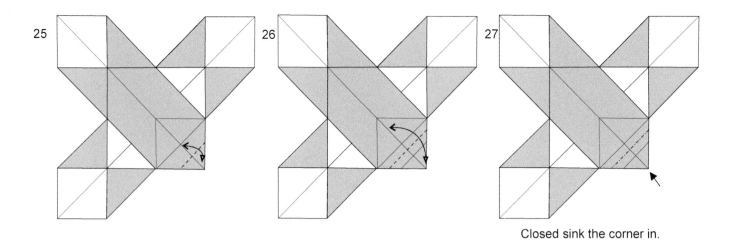

25

26

27

Closed sink the corner in.

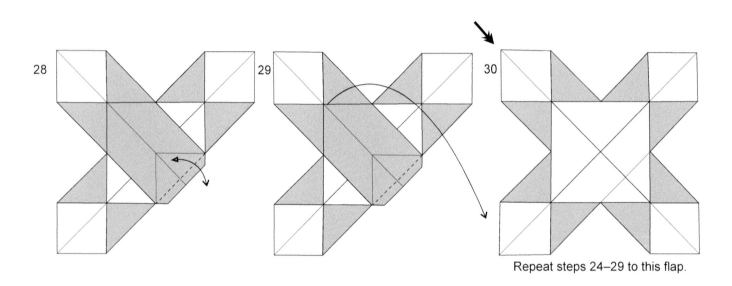

28

29

30

Repeat steps 24–29 to this flap.

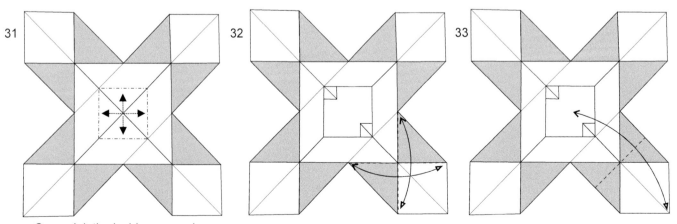

31

Open sink the inside corners in.

32

33

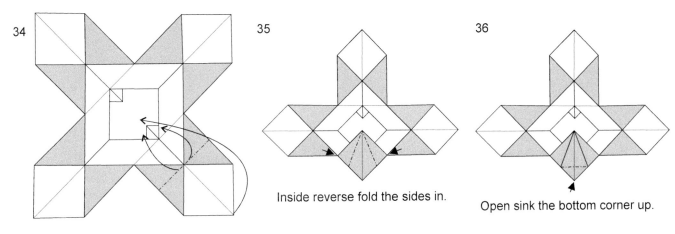

34

Form a preliminary fold from the flap.

35

Inside reverse fold the sides in.

36

Open sink the bottom corner up.

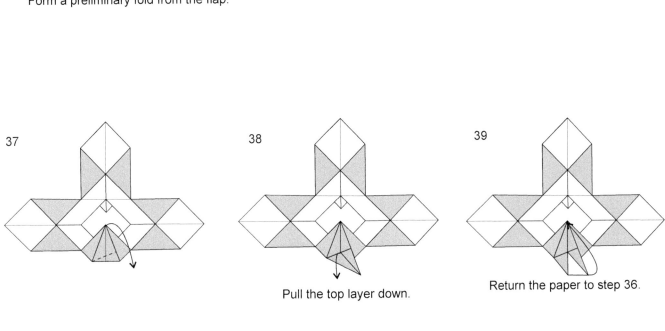

37

38

Pull the top layer down.

39

Return the paper to step 36.

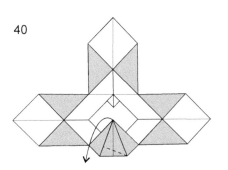

40

Repeat steps 36–38 in the opposite
direction.

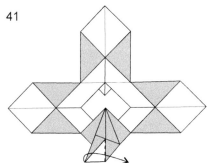

41

Swivel fold the flap over.

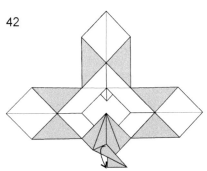

42

Pull the top layer down.

43

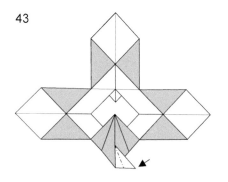

Squash fold the flap down.

44

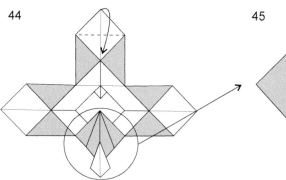

The next sequence of steps will focus on the area circled.

45

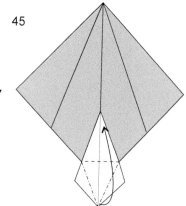

Petal fold the flap up.

46

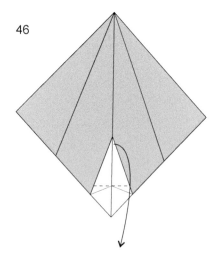

47

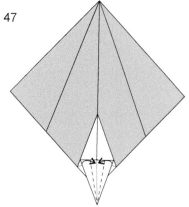

Swivel fold the edges in.

48

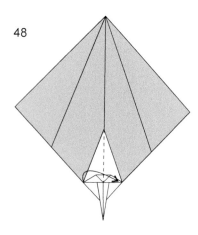

49

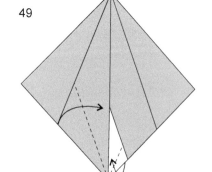

50

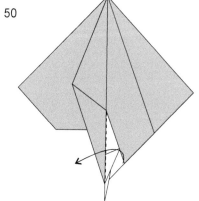

51

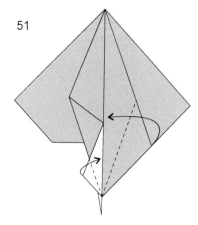

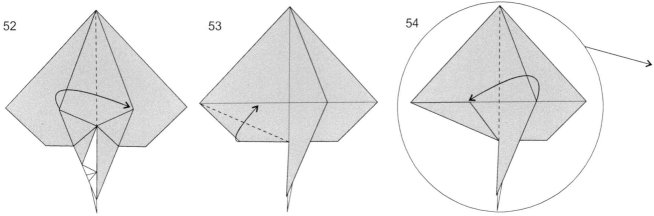

52

53

54

The next sequence of steps will focus back on the rest of the model.

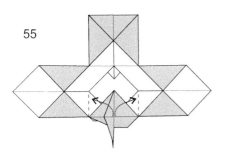

55

Swivel fold the inside corners out.

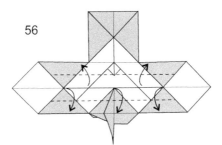

56

57

Turn the model over.

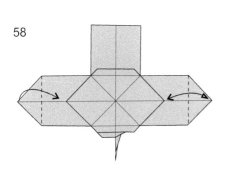

58

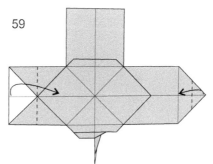

59

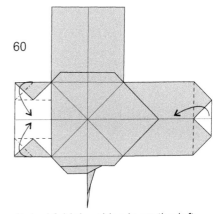

60

Swivel fold the sides in on the left flap, fold the tip of the right flap over.

61

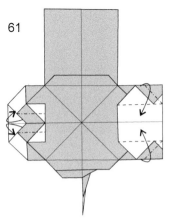

Mountain fold the excess paper underneath on the left flap. Swivel fold the edges on the right flap in.

62

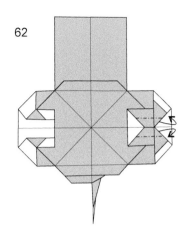

63

Move the excess paper under the flaps below them.

64

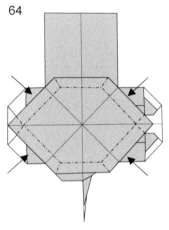

Push in the sides of the model to form the hull, then turn the model over.

65

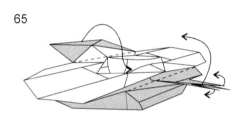

Fold the large flap over so it fits in the pocket on the opposite side. Fold the control tower up, then appropriately position the communications array.

You can open and close the bay door. This ship is capable of floating and carrying many jets, depending on the size of paper used to make it.

66

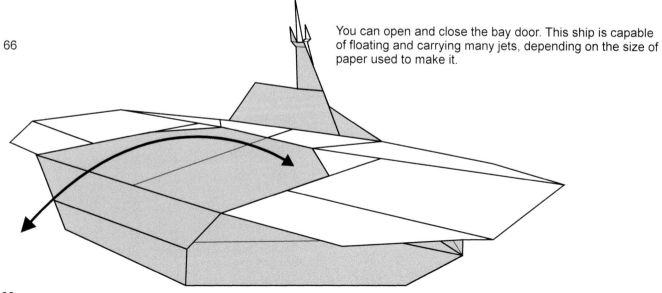

KRAKEN

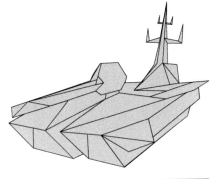

Use a 13-inch-square or larger sheet of foil paper.

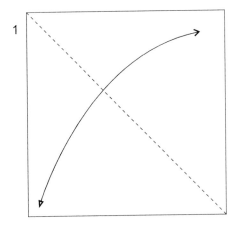

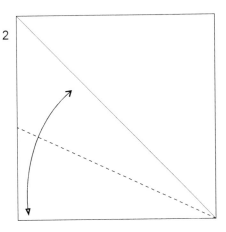

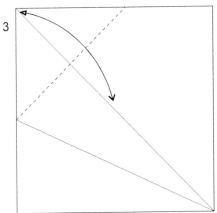

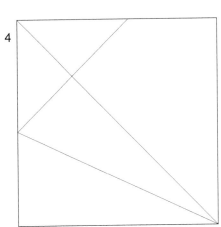

Turn the paper over.

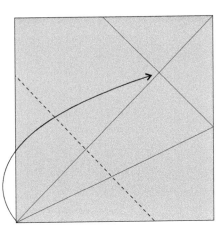

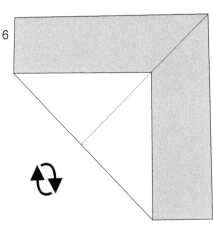

Turn the paper over.

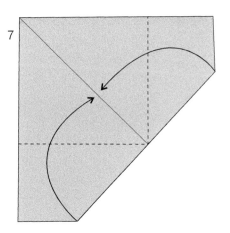

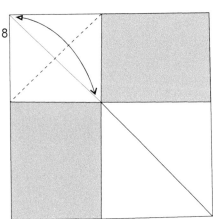

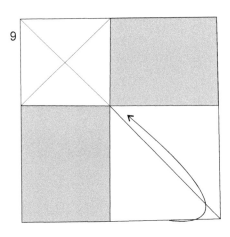

Wrap the paper from behind around and orient the model as shown in step 10.

10

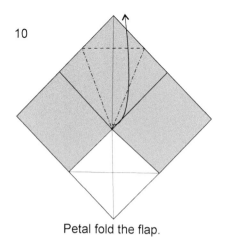

Petal fold the flap.

11

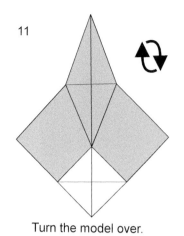

Turn the model over.

12

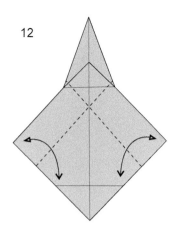

13

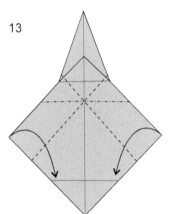

Form a modified preliminary fold
using the creases just made.

14

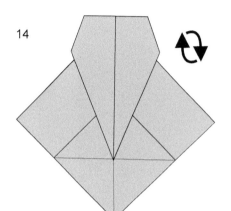

Turn the model over.

15

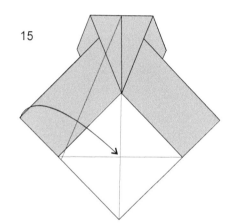

Swivel fold the side over.

16

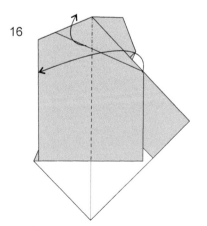

Swivel fold the side over.

17

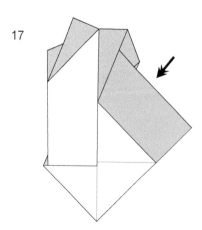

Repeat steps 15–17 to this side.

18

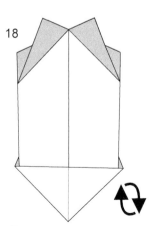

Turn the model over.

19

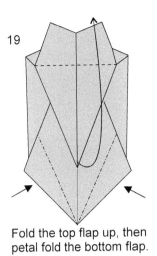

Fold the top flap up, then petal fold the bottom flap.

20

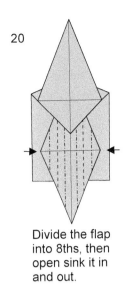

Divide the flap into 8ths, then open sink it in and out.

21

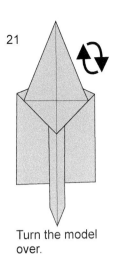

Turn the model over.

22

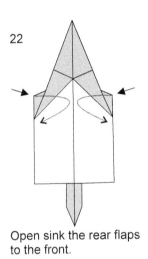

Open sink the rear flaps to the front.

23

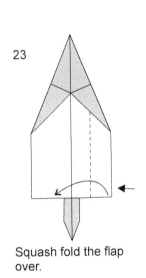

Squash fold the flap over.

24

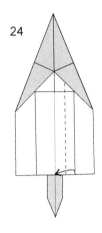

25

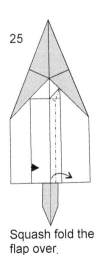

Squash fold the flap over.

26

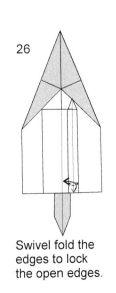

Swivel fold the edges to lock the open edges.

27

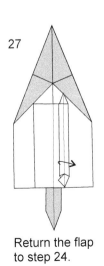

Return the flap to step 24.

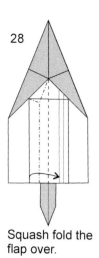

28

Squash fold the
flap over.

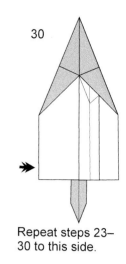

29

Undo the fold
you just made
and position it
to the right.

30

Repeat steps 23–
30 to this side.

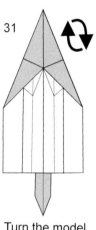

31

Turn the model
over.

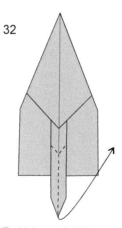

32

Rabbit ear fold the
flap over.

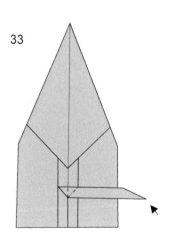

33

Squash fold the flap down.

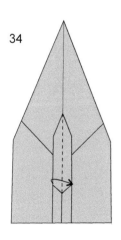

34

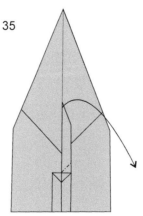

35

Inside reverse fold the
flap.

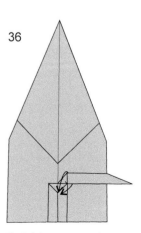

36

Outside reverse fold
the flap as shown.

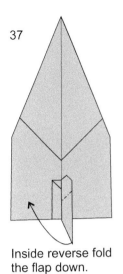

37

Inside reverse fold
the flap down.

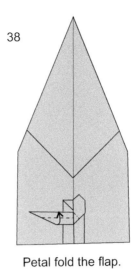

38

Petal fold the flap.

39

Inside reverse fold the
flap.

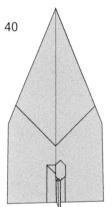

40

Swivel fold both
sides of the flap.

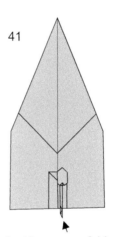

41

Inside reverse fold
the tip in.

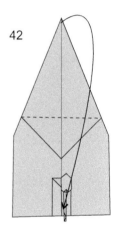

42

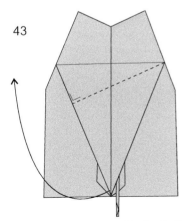

43

Fold the flap perpendicular to itself.

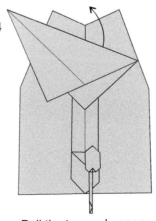

44

Pull the trapped paper
from underneath out as
shown.

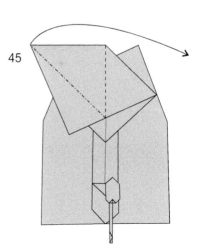

45

Swivel fold the flap over.

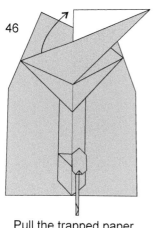

46

Pull the trapped paper
from underneath out.

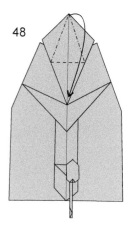

47

Squash fold the flap.

48

Petal fold the flap.

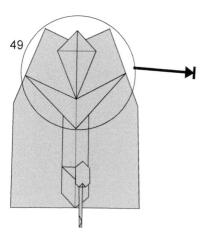

49

The next series of steps will focus
on the area circled.

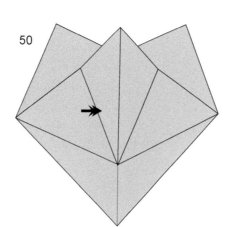

50

Repeat steps 43–49 on this flap.

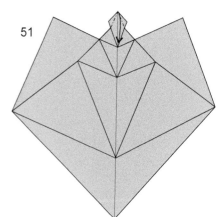

51

Petal fold the small flap.

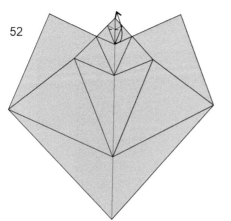

52

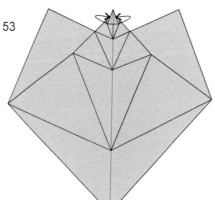

53

Thin the point by swivel folding the
sides in.

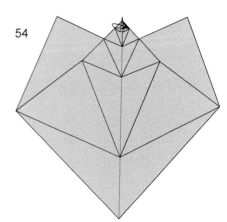

54

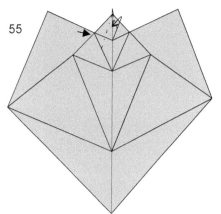

55

Closed sink the left edge in. Valley fold the right edge over.

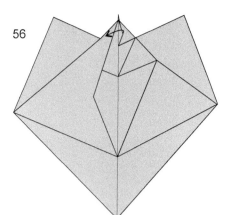

56

Fold two layers over.

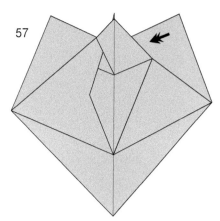

57

Repeat steps 55–57 to this side.

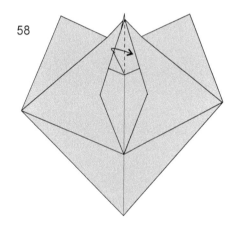

58

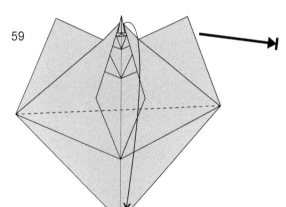

59

Fold the flap down. The remaining set of steps will focus back on the whole model.

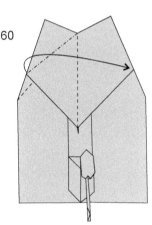

60

Swivel fold the edge over.

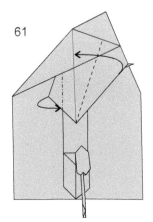

61

Swivel fold the edge over. Mountain fold the area underneath.

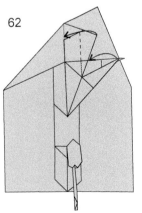

62

Fold the two flaps down. Fold the excess paper down.

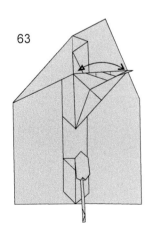

63

Fold then unfold the tips of the flaps up, then unfold them.

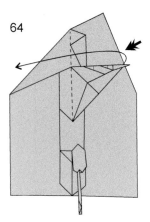

64

Repeat steps 60–64 to the opposite side.

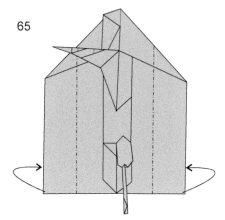

65

Mountain fold the edges behind.

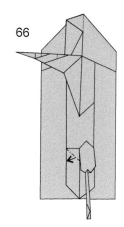

66

Pull the trapped paper from underneath out.

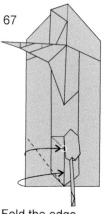

67

Fold the edge over so that it intersects with the area highlighted.

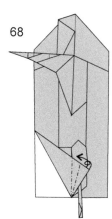

68

Roll the edge over and tuck it into the model.

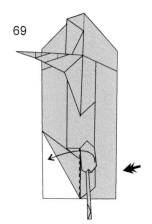

69

Fold the cannon over and repeat steps 66–69 to this side.

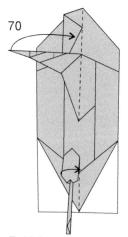

70

Fold the cannon and the bridge up perpendicular.

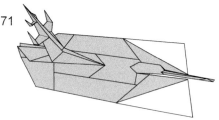

71

Using the creases made in steps 23–31, fold the four bottom edges down.

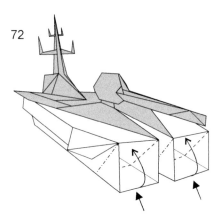

72

Inside reverse fold the edges up. These will become the launch bays.

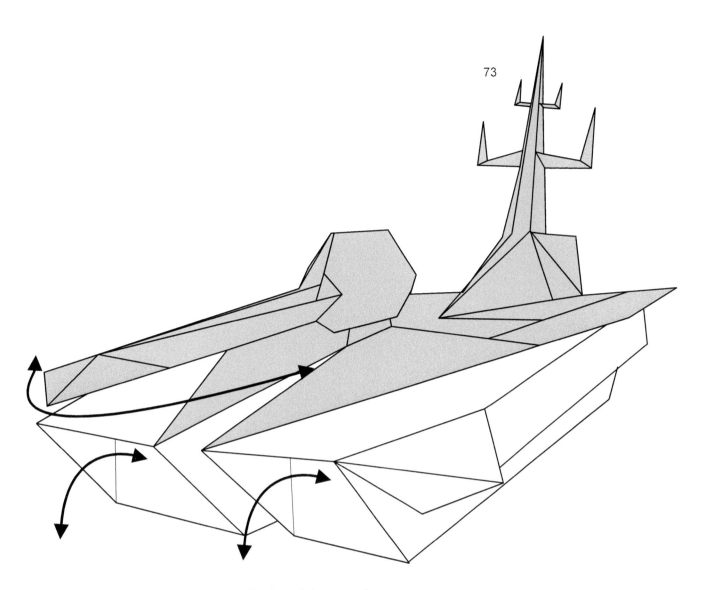

The cannon can swivel 180 degrees. The launch bays can be opened while floating, partially submerging the Kraken in order to launch smaller water craft such as the Triton Gunboat. If you make this ship large enough, it will have room on deck to launch at least two Sabrewolf Helicopters or Valkyrie Dropships.

TRITON GUNBOAT

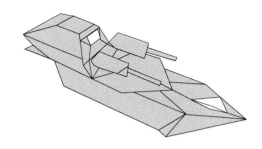

Use a 13-inch-square sheet of foil paper.

1

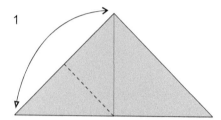

Begin with a waterbomb base. Fold then unfold the flap.

2

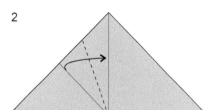

3

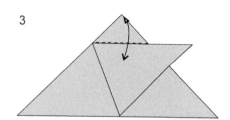

4

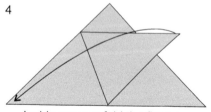

Inside reverse fold the flaps in.

5

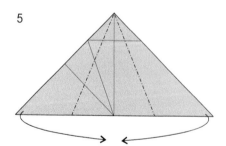

6

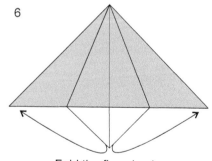

Fold the flaps back.

7

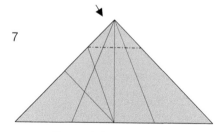

Open sink the point in.

8

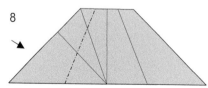

Squash fold the top of the flap and the bottom simultaneously.

9

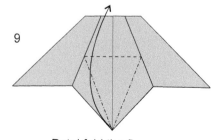

Petal fold the flap up.

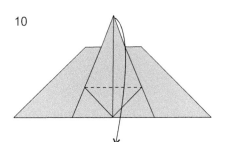

10

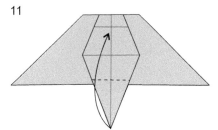

11

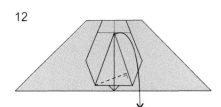

12

Fold the flap perpendicular to itself.

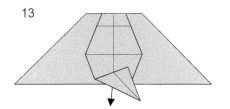

13

Pull the trapped paper out.

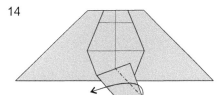

14

Swivel the flap over.

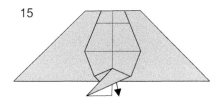

15

Pull the trapped paper out.

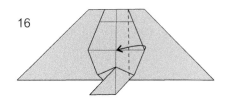

16

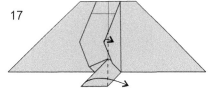

17

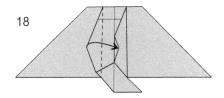

18

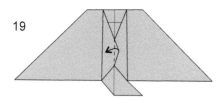

19

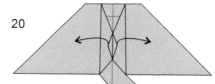

20

Return the model to step 16.

21

Open sink the edges in and out.

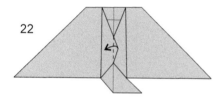

22

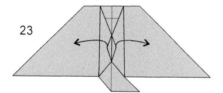

23

Return the model to step 16.

24

Open sink the edges in and out.

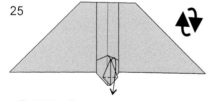

25

Fold the flap down, then turn the model over.

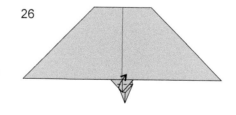

26

27

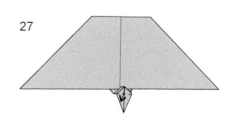

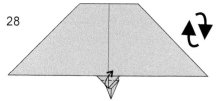

28

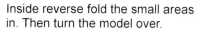

Inside reverse fold the small areas in. Then turn the model over.

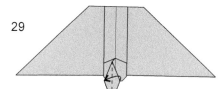

29

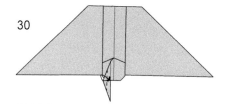

30

Fold the edge over, repeat behind.

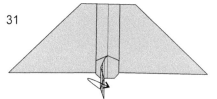

31

Fold the edge over, repeat behind.

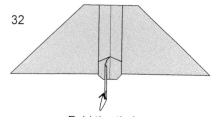

32

Fold the tip in.

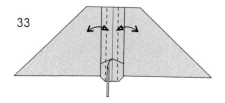

33

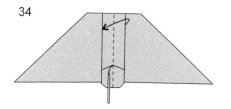

34

35

Repeat steps 8–35 on this side.

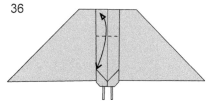

36

Fold and unfold the middle only.

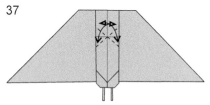

37

Fold and unfold the middle only.

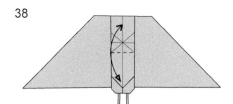

38

39

Using the creases just made, push in the center and then collapse the central area.

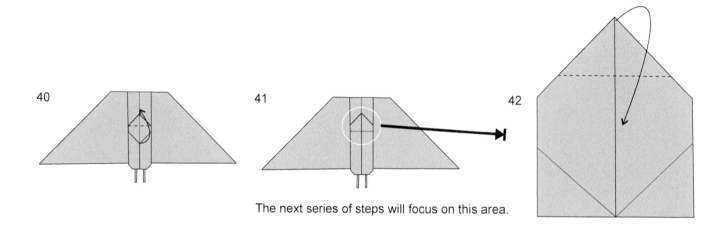

40

41

The next series of steps will focus on this area.

42

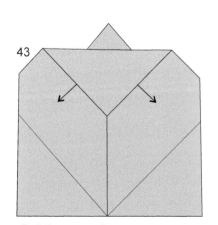

43

Pull the paper from underneath out.

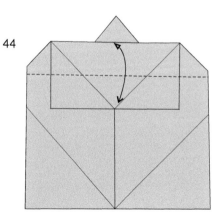

44

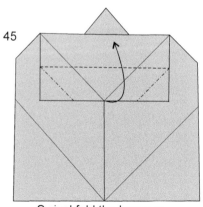

45

Swivel fold the layer up.

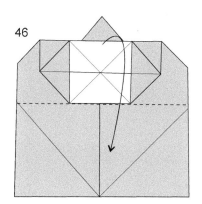

46

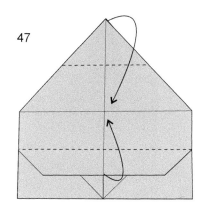

47

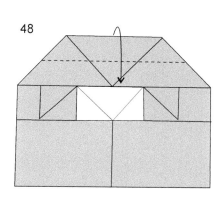

48

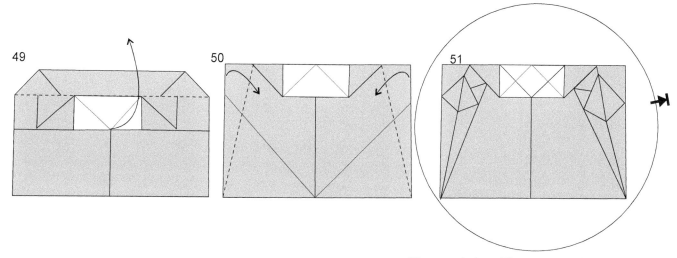

49

50

51

The remainder of the steps will focus back on the rest of the model.

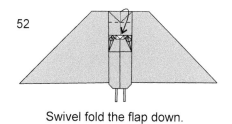

52

Swivel fold the flap down.

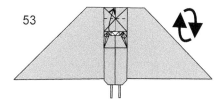

53

Fold the flap back up, then turn the model over.

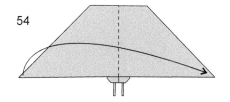

54

55

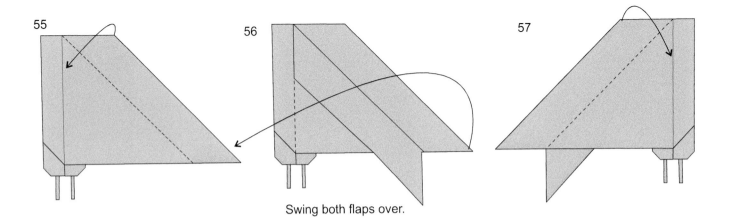

56

Swing both flaps over.

57

58

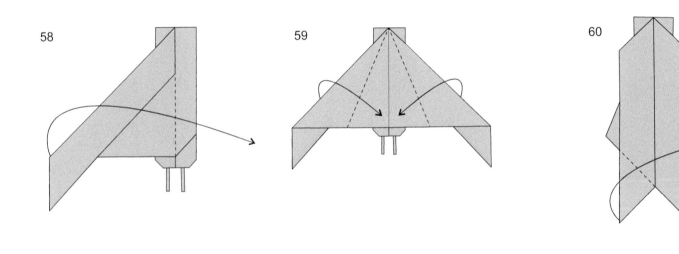

59

60

61

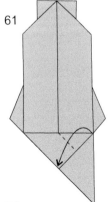

62

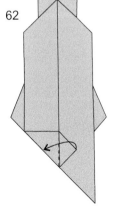

63

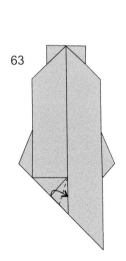

64

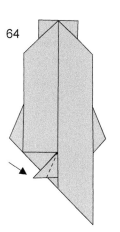

Squash fold the flap.

65

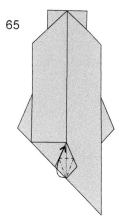

Petal fold the flap up.

66

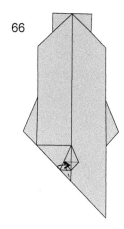

67

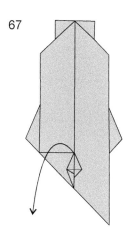

Return the flap to step 60.

68

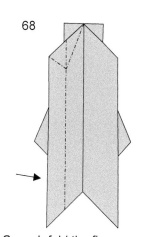

Squash fold the flap over.

69

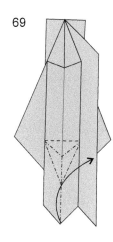

Using the creases, squash fold the flap over.

70

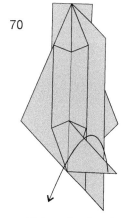

Return the flap to step 68.

71

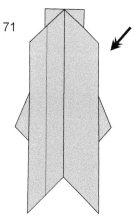

Repeat steps 60–70 to this flap.

72

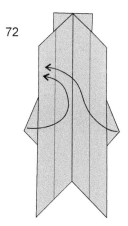

Pull the paper from underneath out.

73

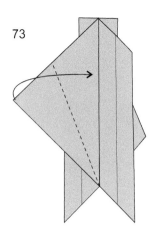

74

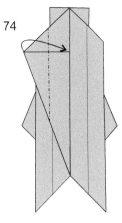

Inside reverse fold
the edge in.

75

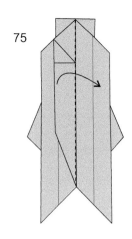

76

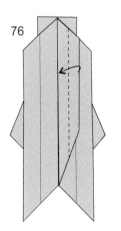

77

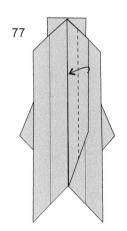

78

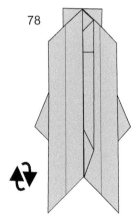

Turn the model over.

79

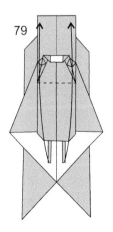

80

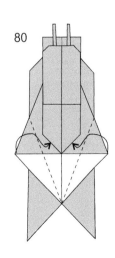

81

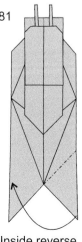

Inside reverse
fold the flap in.

82

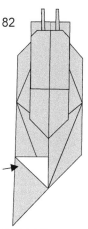

Refold the
creases made
in steps 60–67.

83

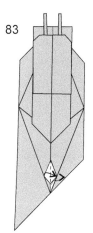

Fold the top flap
over, then tuck in
the bottom edge only.

84

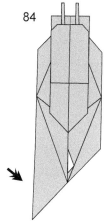

Repeat this
process to this
flap.

85

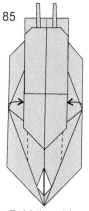

Fold the sides
underneath.

86

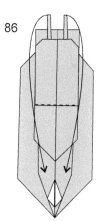

87

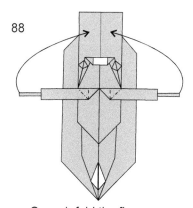

Rabbit ear fold the
flaps out.

88

Squash fold the flaps up.

89

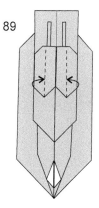

Fold the flaps
in half so they
stand upright.

90

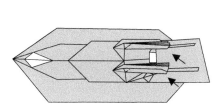

Squash fold the flaps up.

91

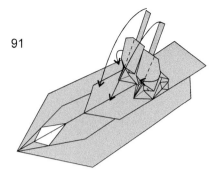

Outside reverse fold the flaps down.

92

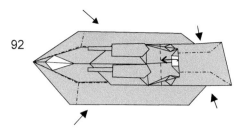

Push in the sides of the top area to form a bridge. Using the creases, push in the bottom of the boat to form a hull.

93

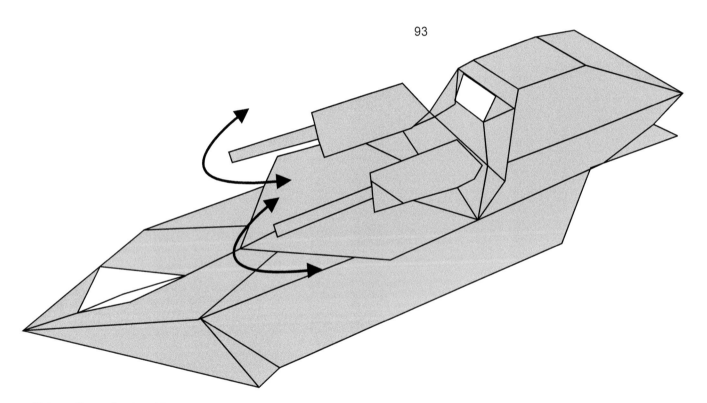

This craft can float and it can carry two missiles on the forward flaps. The gun turrets can swivel to a great degree.

VANGUARD TRANSFORMER

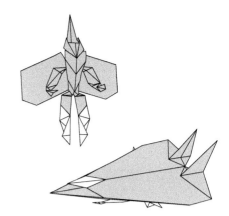

Use a 10-inch-square sheet of paper.

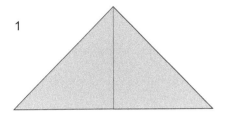

1

Begin with a waterbomb base.

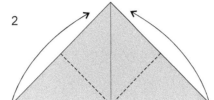

2

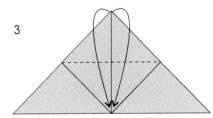

3

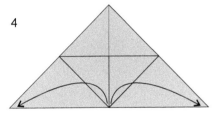

4

Fold the flaps back to step 2.

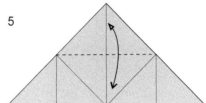

5

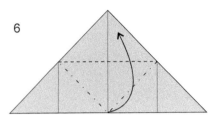

6

Using the creases made, petal fold the flap up.

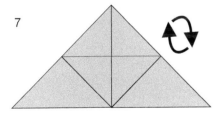

7

Turn the model over.

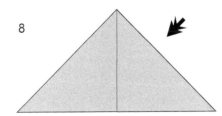

8

Repeat steps 1–7 to this side.

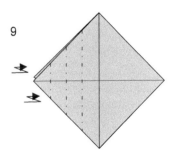

9

Open sink both edges in as shown.

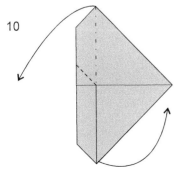

10

Swivel fold the top flap over and simultaneously swivel fold the bottom flap over as shown.

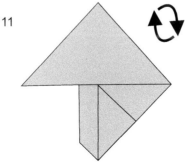

11

Turn the model over.

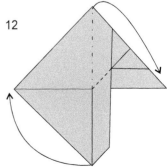

12

Swivel fold the top flap over and simultaneously swivel fold the bottom flap over as shown.

13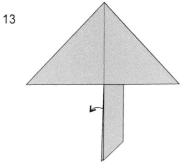

Fold the rear flap over as shown.

14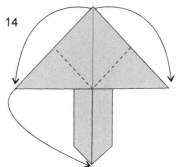

Fold the area out as shown in step 15.

15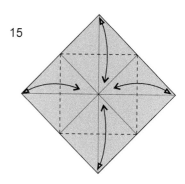

16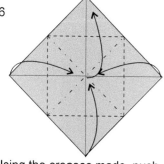

Using the creases made, push the central area up and fold the sides in.

17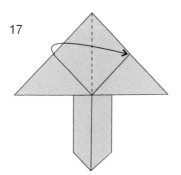

18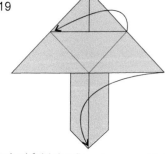

Open sink the area in.

19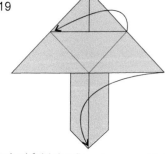

Swivel fold the flap down and fold the edge over.

20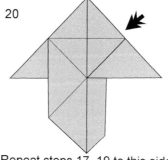

Repeat steps 17–19 to this side.

21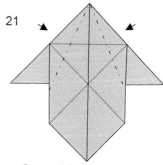

Open sink the sides in.

22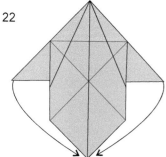

Swivel the flaps down.

23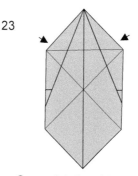

Open sink the sides in.

24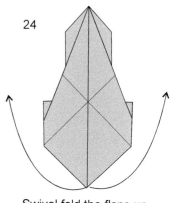

Swivel fold the flaps up.

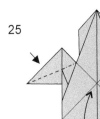

25

Fold the bottom flaps up
and inside reverse fold the
side flaps in.

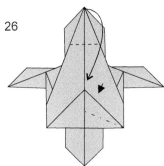

26

Valley fold the top flap down.
Squash fold the bottom flap.

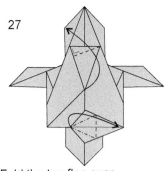

27

Fold the top flap over
perpendicular to itself as shown.
Petal fold the bottom flap over.

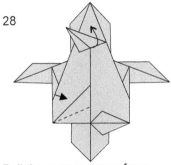

28

Pull the excess paper from
the top flap out. Squash fold
the bottom flap.

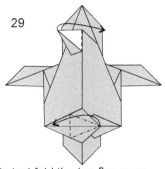

29

Swivel fold the top flap over.
Petal fold the bottom flap over.

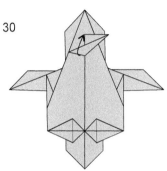

30

Pull the excess paper from
underneath out.

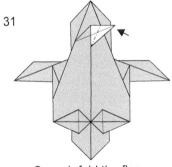

31

Squash fold the flap.

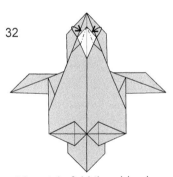

32

Mountain fold the sides in.

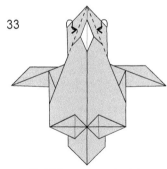

33

Fold the edges inside.

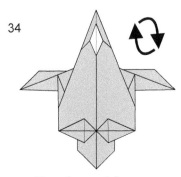

34

Turn the model over.

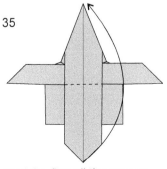

35

Fold the flap all the way up.

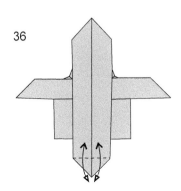

36

37

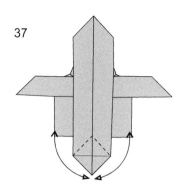

38

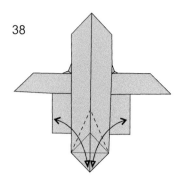

39

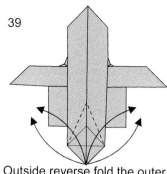

Outside reverse fold the outer layers using the creases.

40

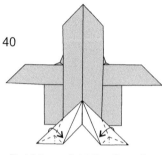

Rabbit ear fold the flaps in.

41

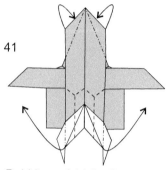

Rabbit ear fold the flaps up.
Mountain fold the edges in.

42

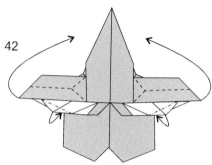

Rabbit ear fold the flaps up.
Mountain fold the small edges in as shown.

43

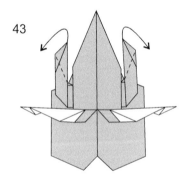

44

Squash fold the small flaps.

45

Petal fold the small flaps up.

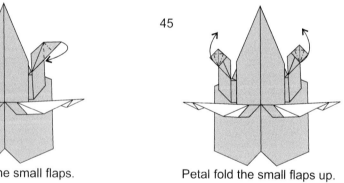

46

Mountain fold the edges behind.
Then mountain fold the bottom flaps in.

47

Fold the points shown so they stand upright, then turn the model over.

48

Fold the tailfins up.

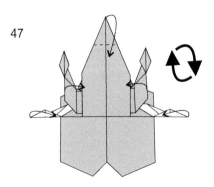

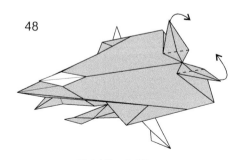

49

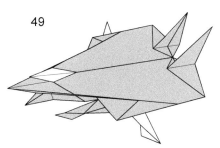

Jet mode complete. Continue to step 49 to configure flight mode. Continue to step 52 to transform to robot mode.

50

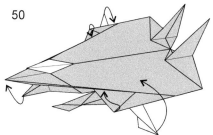

Fold the edges of the wings in, then fold the landing gear in as well. Fold the front landing strut up.

51

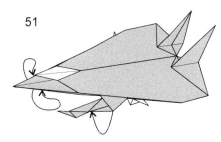

Fold the arms in. Fold the edges from the front landing strut in to lock it into place.

52

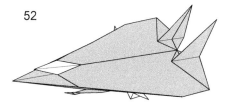

The "hands" can be used to attach missiles and guns to. The craft can fly.

53

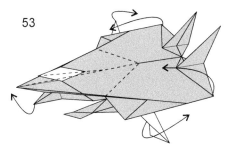

Fold the model in half, fold the wings up. Swing the rear landing struts back. Use step 54 as a reference.

54

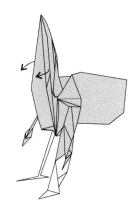

Fold the edges out.

55

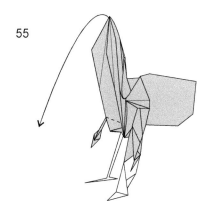

Inside reverse fold the flap down.

56

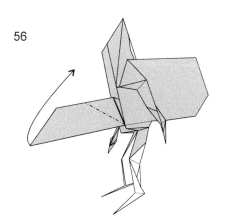

Inside reverse fold the flap up.

57

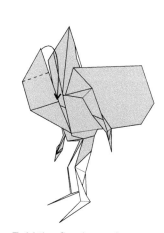

Fold the flap inward.

58

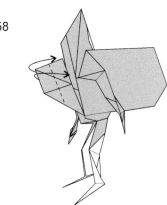

Valley fold the edges in.

59

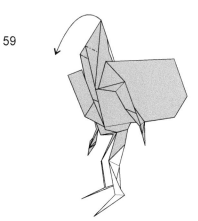

Inside reverse fold the inner flap out.

60

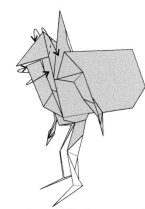

First wrap the middle flap around to form the torso, then outside reverse fold the top flap to form the head.

61

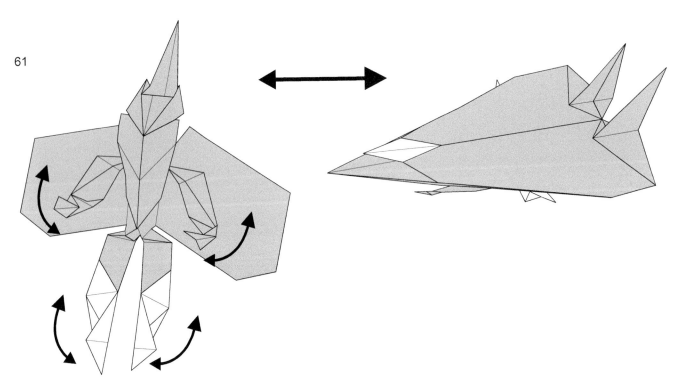

You can pose the arms and legs and it can carry weapons or missiles. To transform it back into jet mode, simply reverse the folding process to step 53.

PHALANX

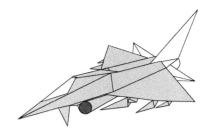

Use a 13-inch-square sheet of foil paper.

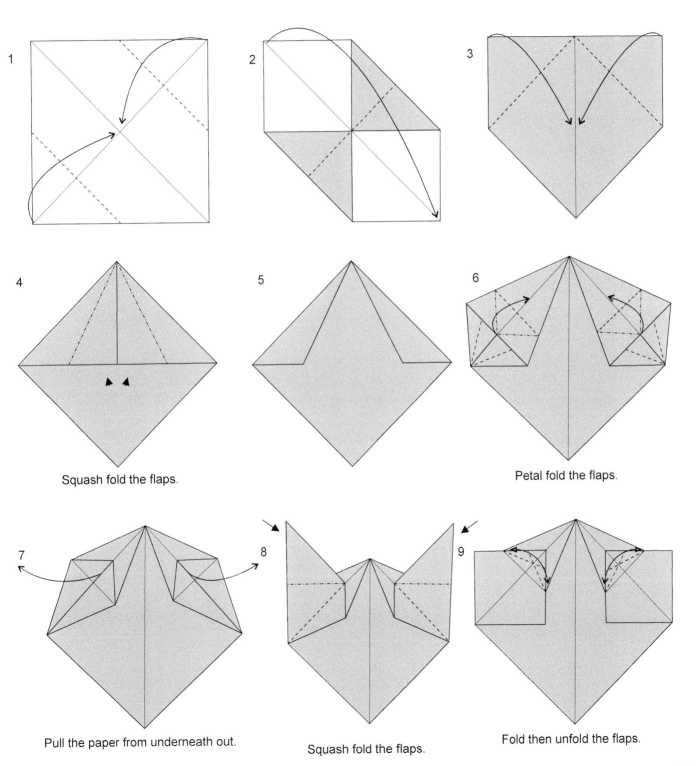

1

2

3

4

Squash fold the flaps.

5

6

Petal fold the flaps.

7

Pull the paper from underneath out.

8

Squash fold the flaps.

9

Fold then unfold the flaps.

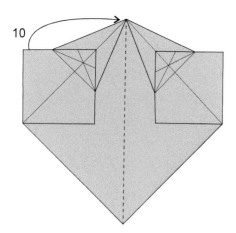

10

Fold the model in half.

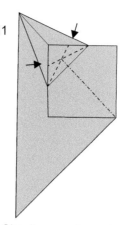

11

Simultaneously push the top of the triangle in and move the sides out. Repeat behind.

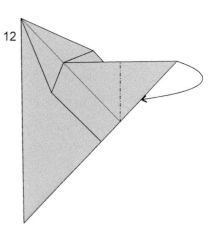

12

Inside reverse fold the flap. Repeat behind.

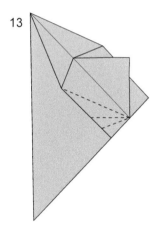

13

Make the creases shown. Repeat behind.

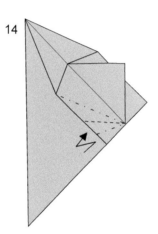

14

Inside reverse fold the edge in and out. Repeat behind.

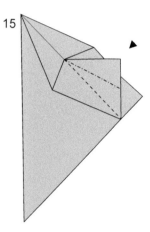

15

Squash fold the flap. Repeat behind.

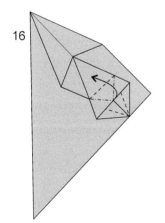

16

Petal fold the flap. Repeat behind.

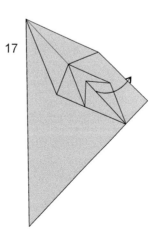

17

Pull the paper from underneath out. Repeat behind.

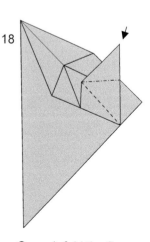

18

Squash fold the flap down. Repeat behind.

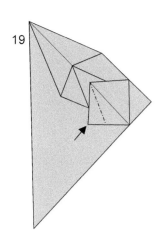

19

Inside reverse fold the
edge. Repeat behind.

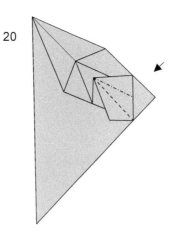

20

Squash fold the flap
down. Repeat
behind.

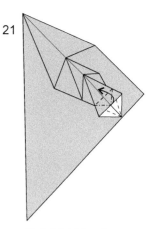

21

Petal fold the flap.
Repeat behind.

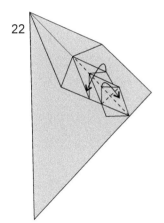

22

First fold the small
triangle down, then
fold the layers over.
Repeat behind.

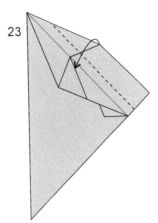

23

Fold the edge down
as shown. Repeat
behind.

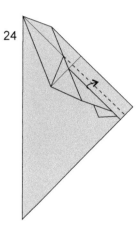

24

Fold the edge up
as shown. Repeat
behind.

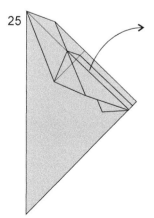

25

Unfold the edge to
step 23. Repeat
behind.

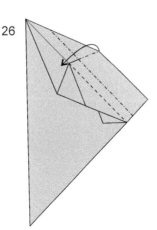

26

Using the creases
just made, spread the
paper out.

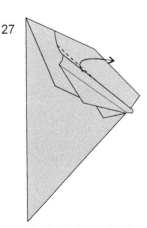

27

Push the layer back
and flatten all of it
except the front.

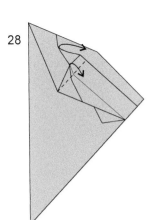

28

Fold the point back
and flatten the
paper out.

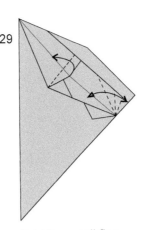

29

Fold the small flap
over. Fold then unfold
the edge as shown.

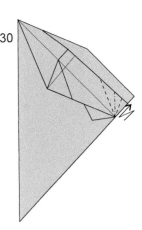

30

Inside reverse fold
both layers in and out.

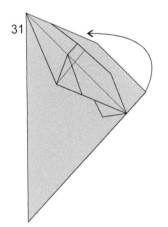

31

Fold the model out.

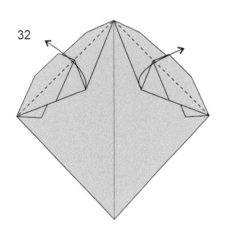

32

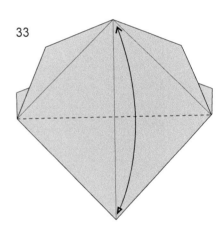

33

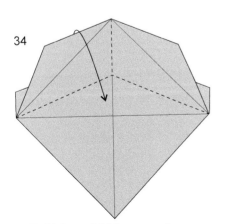

34

Rabbit ear fold the area shown.

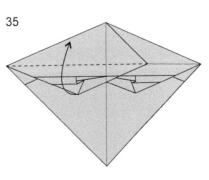

35

36

Fold the middle flap over, then fold
the other layers up.

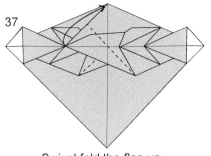

37

Swivel fold the flap up.

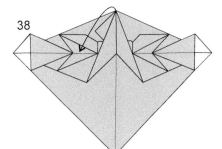

38

Return the flap to step 37.

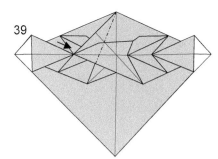

39

Squash fold the flap.

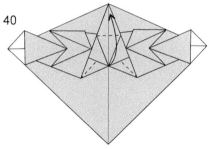

40

Petal fold the flap up, then spread the bottom edges out.

41

Fold then unfold the layer, then turn the model over.

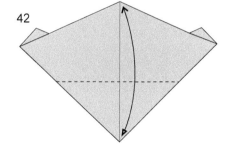

42

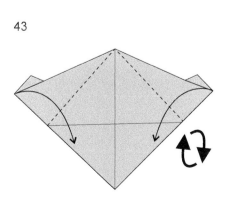

43

Fold the sides in, then turn the model over.

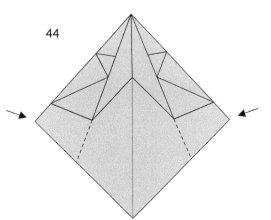

44

Inside reverse fold the sides in.

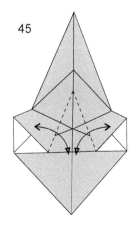

45

46

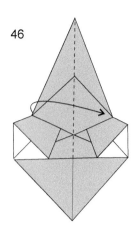

47

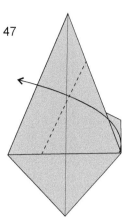

Using the crease made in step 45, fold the flap over. The model will not lie flat.

48

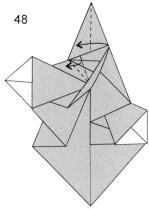

Crimp the edge shown and fold the paper back over.

49

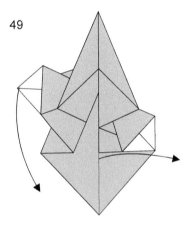

Open out the model as shown in step 50.

50

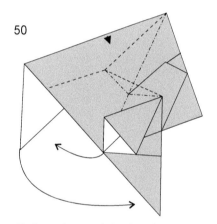

Reform the model using the creases shown. You are basically moving the crimp made in step 49 to free both layers of paper.

51

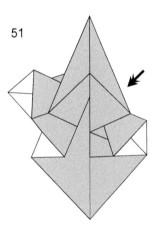

Repeat steps 48–50 to this side.

52

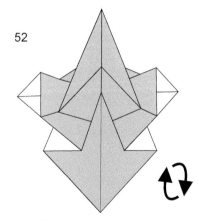

Turn the model over.

53

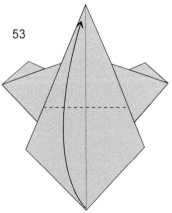

Petal fold the flap. Note you will also have to swivel fold the bottom edges.

54

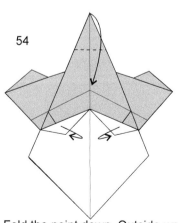

Fold the point down. Outside wrap the bottom area shown.

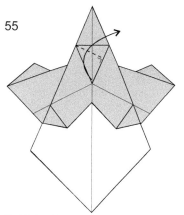

55

Fold the flap perpendicular to itself.

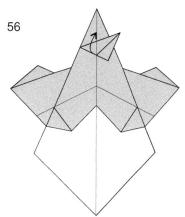

56

Pull the trapped paper down.

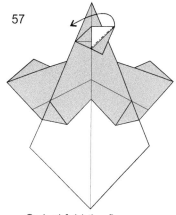

57

Swivel fold the flap over.

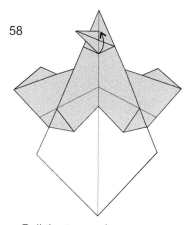

58

Pull the trapped paper out.

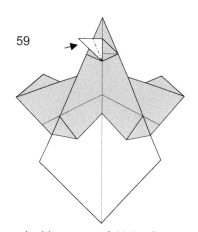

59

Inside reverse fold the flap.

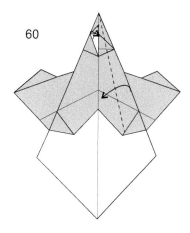

60

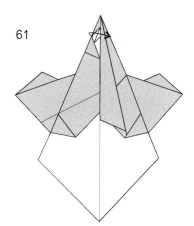

61

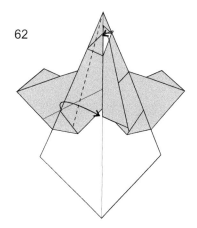

62

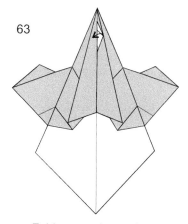

63

Fold over only one layer.

64

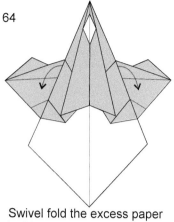

Swivel fold the excess paper inside down.

65

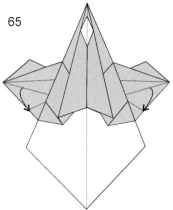

Reposition the inner flaps by swivel folding them down slightly and line them up using the creases shown.

66

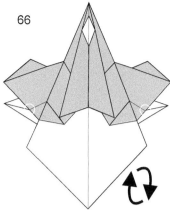

Note the intersections. You will have to turn the model over to complete this fold.

67

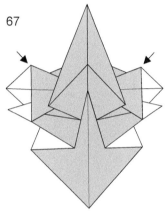

While performing the folds in the previous steps, do not allow the edges shown to move.

68

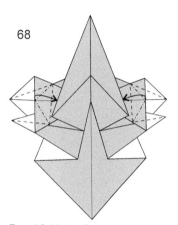

Petal fold the flaps as shown.

69

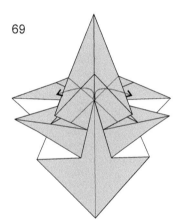

Fold the inner flaps out.

70

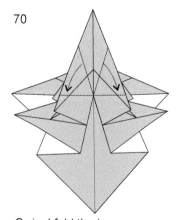

Swivel fold the inner excess paper over.

71

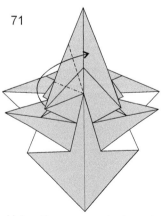

Using the creases just made, swivel the layer of paper over.

72

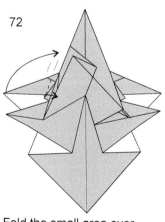

Fold the small area over, then inside reverse fold the large flap perpendicular to the edge of the large triangle.

73

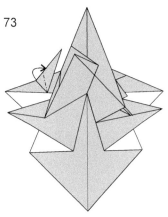

Fold the small edge in.

74

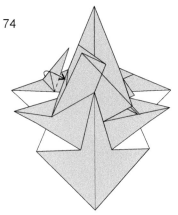

Fold the edge of the flap over.
You will have to swivel fold the
other side to lay it flat.

75

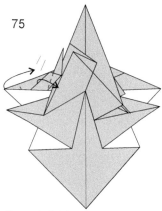

Squash fold the small triangle,
then inside reverse fold the
large flap perpendicular to the
edge of the large triangle over.

76

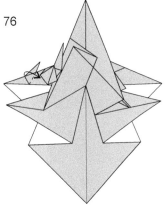

Fold the edge of the flap over.
You will have to swivel fold the
other side to lay it flat.

77

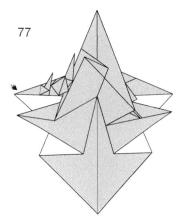

78

Repeat steps 75–77 to the
last flap.

79

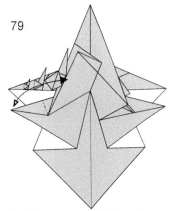

Inside reverse fold the flap over,
then fold it back.

80

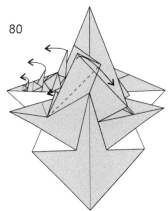

Fold all of the flaps on the wing
over. Fold the large triangle
area as shown.

81

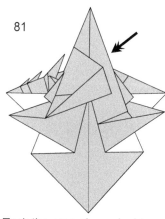

Tuck the area shown inside
the model, then repeat steps
71–81 to the other side.

82

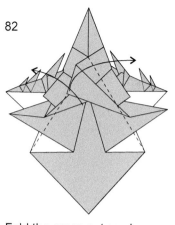

Fold the areas out as shown.

83

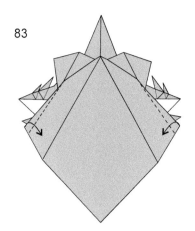

84

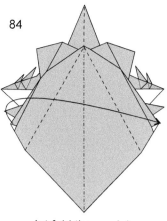

Jet fold the model.

85

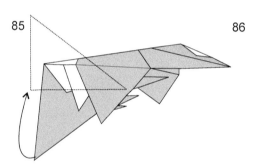

Using the crease made in step 41 as a guide, inside reverse fold the flap up.

86

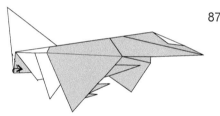

Fold both layers over.

87

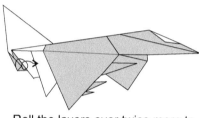

Roll the layers over twice more to lock the model together.

88

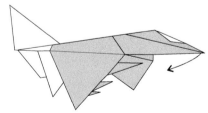

Inside reverse fold the flap down.

89

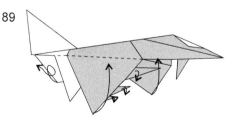

To finish the model fold the wings up, fold all of the missile racks down, roll the paper in the back to form afterburners, roll the paper in the front up to form air intakes, and fold the rear landing gear down.

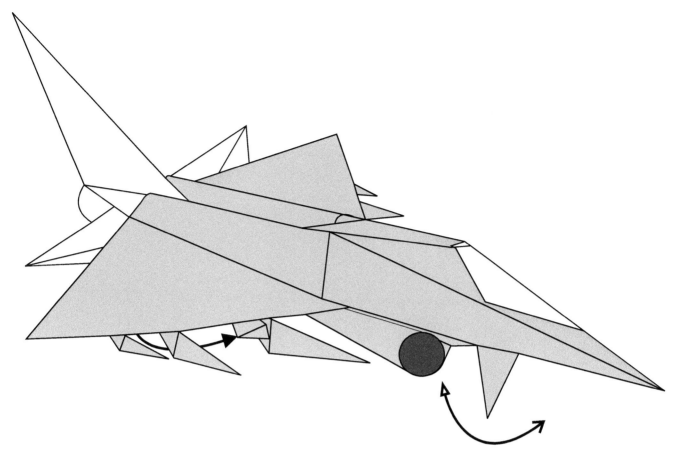

To fly this aircraft inside, reverse fold the landing gear and grab the keel.
Give this aircraft a strong throw. This jet can carry up to eight missiles
using the missile racks.

VALKYRIE DROPSHIP

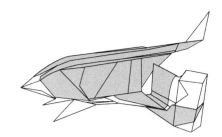

Use a 13-inch-square sheet of foil paper.

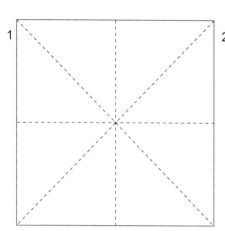

Make the creases shown.

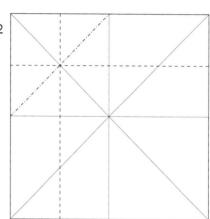

Rabbit ear fold the paper as shown.

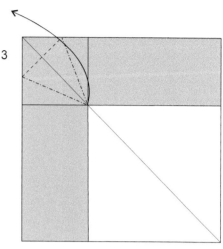

Petal fold the flap.

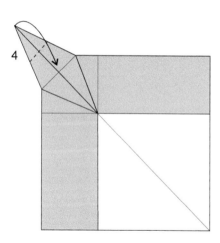

Fold the flap over perpendicular to itself as shown.

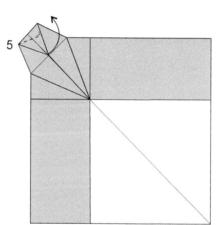

Pull the trapped paper out.

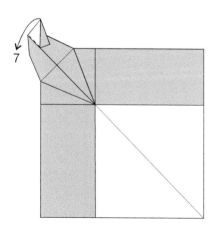

Swivel fold the flap over.

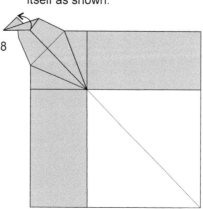

Pull the trapped paper out.

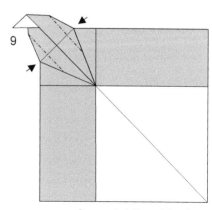

Open sink the sides in.

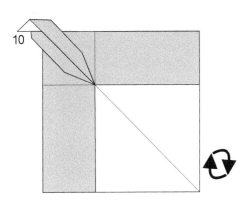

Turn the model over.

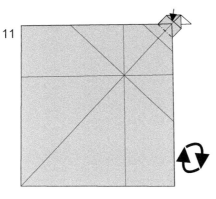

Closed sink the corner in.

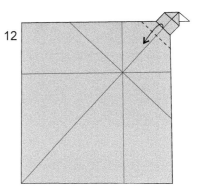

Fold the flap down, then turn the model over.

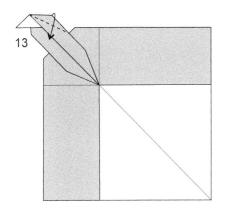

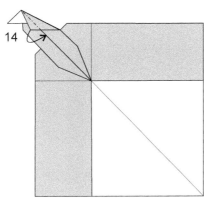

Mountain fold the edge behind as shown.

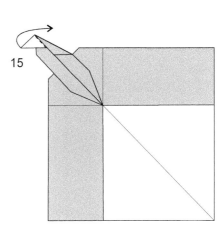

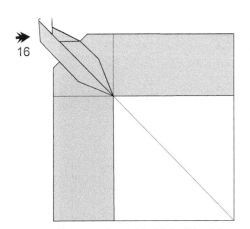

Repeat steps 11–13 to this side.

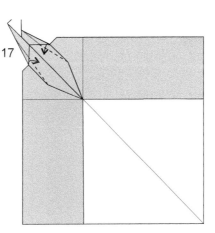

Fold the sides in.

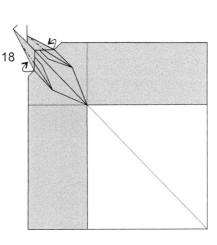

Fold the edges behind.

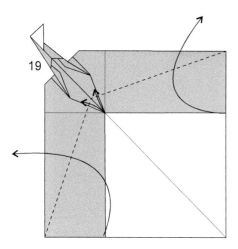
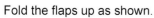

19

Fold the flaps up as shown.

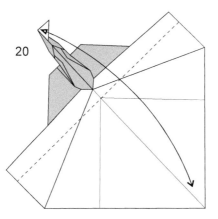

20

Fold then unfold the model.

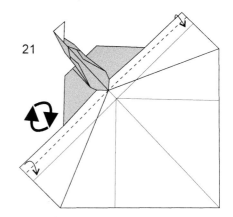

21

Fold the edges down, then turn the model over.

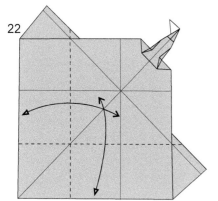

22

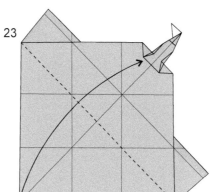

23

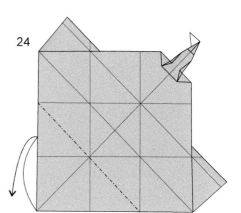

24

Mountain fold the flap behind, then unfold.

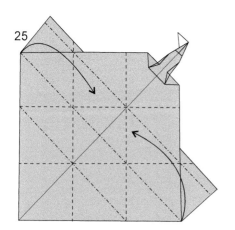

25

Using the creases made, perform a double rabbit ear fold.

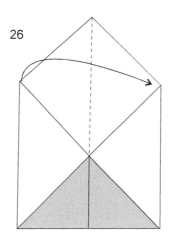

26

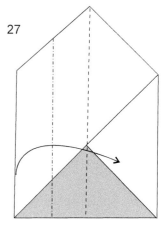

27

Squash fold the flap over.

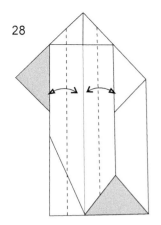

28

Fold then unfold the sides.

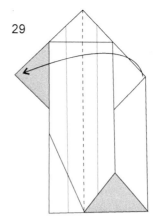

29

Fold three layers of paper over.

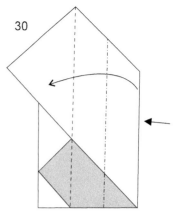

30

Squash fold the flap over.

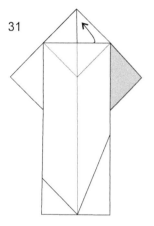

31

Pull the center paper up.

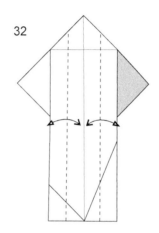

32

Fold then unfold the sides.

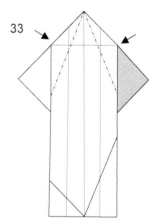

33

Open sink the sides in, repeat behind.

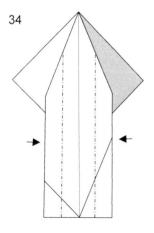

34

Open sink the sides in.

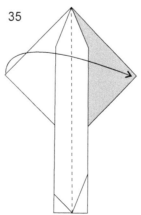

35

Fold the layers over.

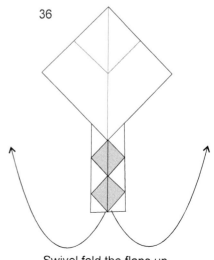

36

Swivel fold the flaps up.

37

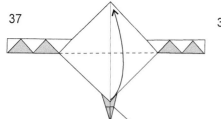

38

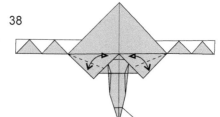

39

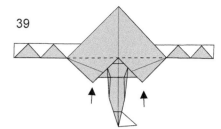

Inside reverse fold the flaps up.

40

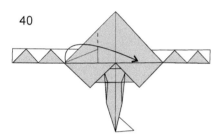
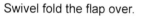

Swivel fold the flap over.

41

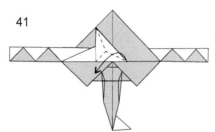

Rabbit ear fold the flap.

42

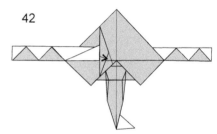

Swivel fold the bottom layers over as shown.

43

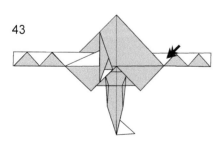

Repeat steps 38–41 to this side.

44

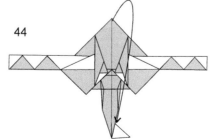

Unfold to step 36.

45

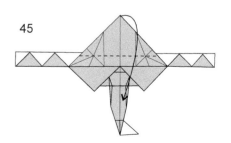

Fold the flap down as shown.

46

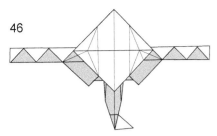

Refold the creases made in step 36.

47

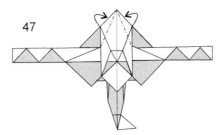

Mountain fold the edges behind as shown.

48

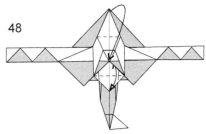

Fold one flap down.

49

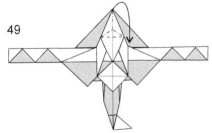

Rabbit ear fold the flap down.

50

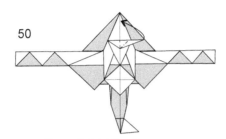

Squash fold the flap up.

51

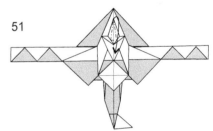

Petal fold the flap down.

52

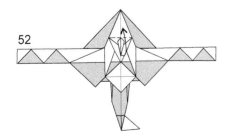

Fold the flap up.

53

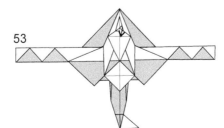

Fold the small triangle down as shown.

54

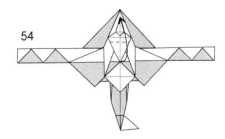

Fold the flap up.

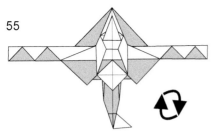

55

Turn the model over.

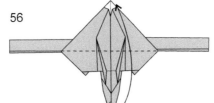

56

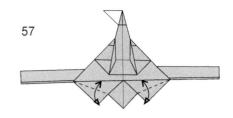

57

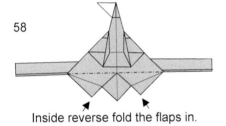

58

Inside reverse fold the flaps in.

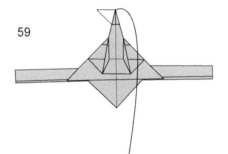

59

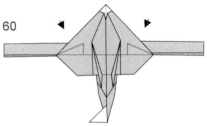

60

Using the creases made in step 56, inside reverse fold the edges in.

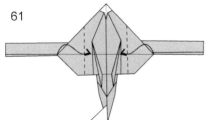

61

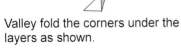

Valley fold the corners under the layers as shown.

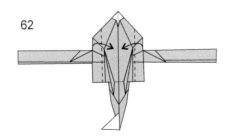

62

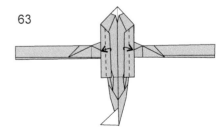

63

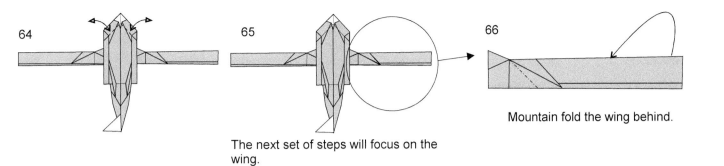

64

65

The next set of steps will focus on the wing.

66

Mountain fold the wing behind.

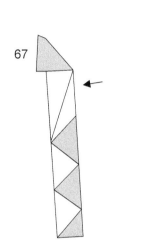

67

Closed sink the pleat around.

68

Fold then unfold the wing as shown.

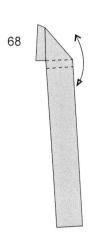

69

Squash fold the flap over.

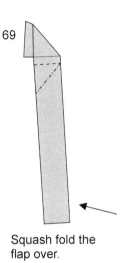

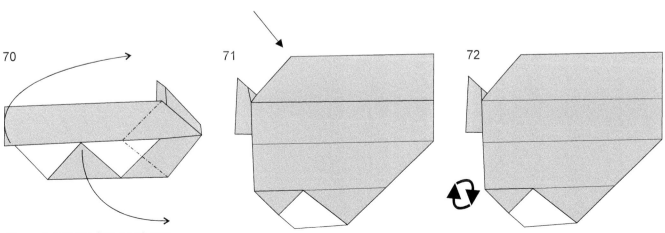

70

Squash fold the flap as shown.

71

Closed sink the edges around.

72

Turn the model over.

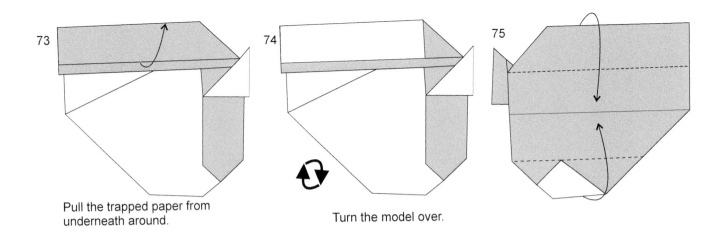

73 Pull the trapped paper from underneath around.

74 Turn the model over.

75

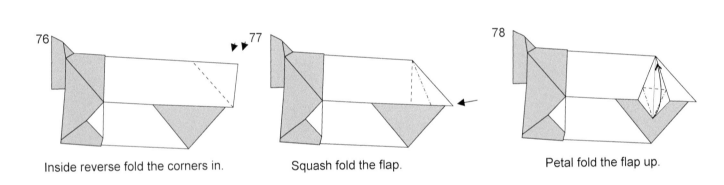

76 Inside reverse fold the corners in.

77 Squash fold the flap.

78 Petal fold the flap up.

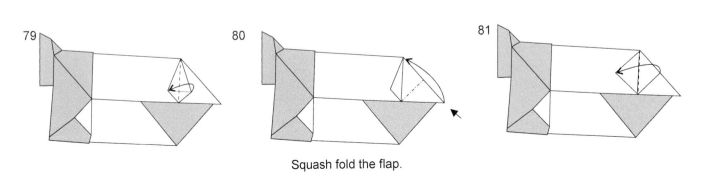

79

80 Squash fold the flap.

81

82

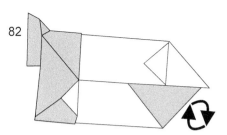

Turn the model over.

83

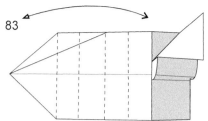

Make the valley folds as shown.

84

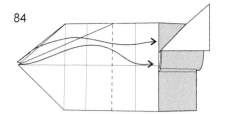

Fold the flap over and place the large triangle all the way inside. Place the small triangle in the corresponding pocket. The remaining steps will focus on the rest of the model.

85

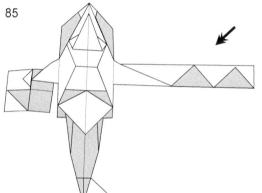

Repeat steps 62–81 to this wing.

86

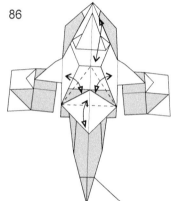

Fold then unfold the creases shown. Note these folds will be used to transition between flight mode and landing mode by folding the flaps into the pockets shown. The landing ramp also has a pocket behind it that it will lock into.

87

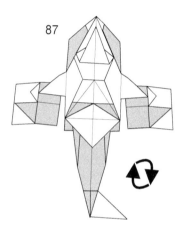

Turn the model over.

88

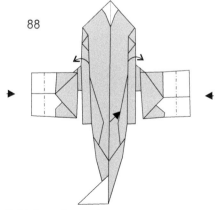

Fold the edges of the wings out to form engines, then pull the top layer up to form the cargo area.

89

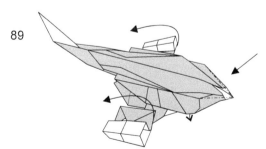

Shape the nose, fold the landing gear down to hold the ship, rotate the engines in landing configuration.

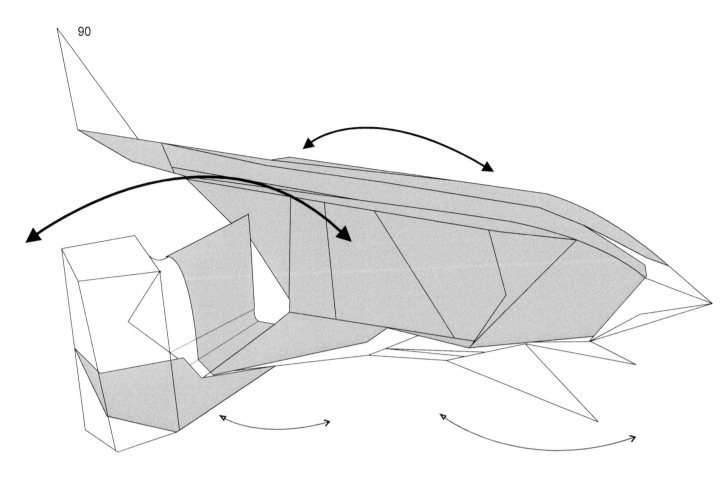

This ship can hold personnel and equipment. The landing gear and ramp can fold and lock into place as described in step 86 to transition to flight mode. The engines can rotate for transport or landing mode. Note the engines also have four hardpoints made in step 83 to carry four missiles.

SABREWOLF

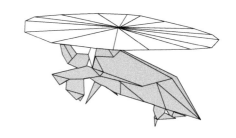

Use a 13-inch-square sheet of foil paper.

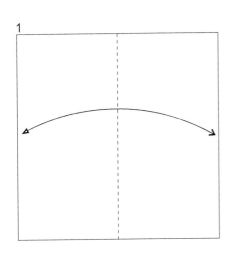

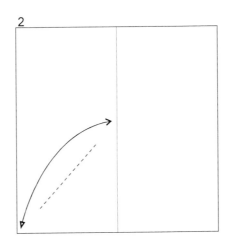

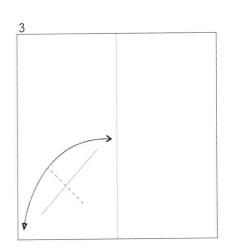

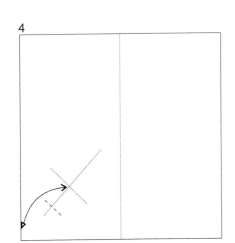

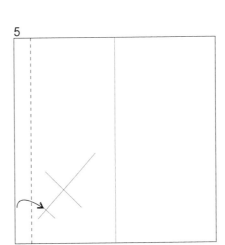

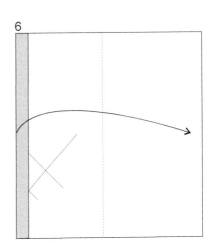

Valley fold the paper inside.

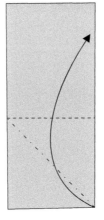

Squash fold the paper over.

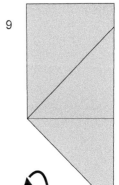

Turn the model over.

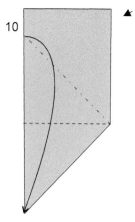

10

Squash fold the flap
down.

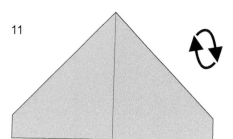

11

Turn the model over.

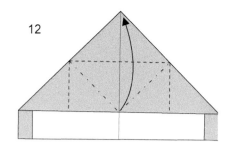

12

Petal fold the flap up.

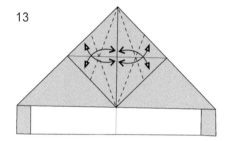

13

Fold then unfold the sides in.

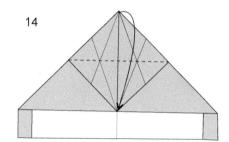

14

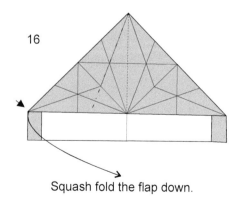

15

Pull the flap from inside out.

16

Squash fold the flap down.

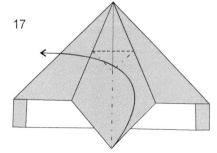

17

Using the creases, squash fold the flap
up.

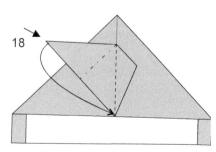

18

Squash fold the flap down.

19

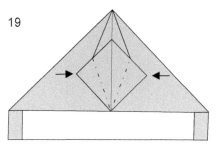

Inside reverse fold the sides in.

20

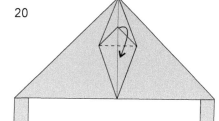

21

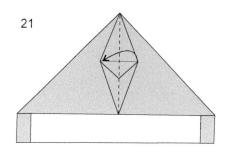

22

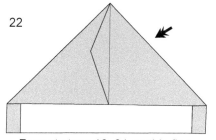

Repeat steps 16–21 on this flap.

23

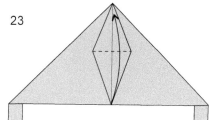

24

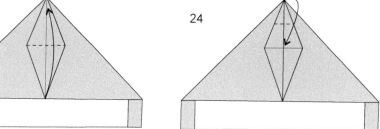

25

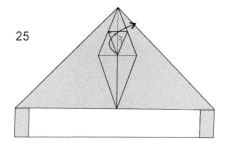

Fold the flap up perpendicular to itself.

26

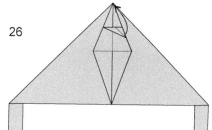

Return the flap to step 24.

27

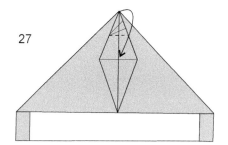

Repeat the process in the opposite direction.

28

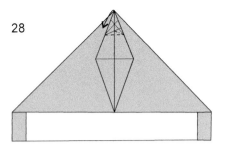

Using the creases you just made, swivel fold the paper down.

29

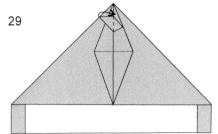

Swivel fold the flap over.

30

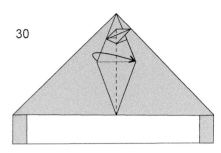

Fold the flap over. This will unlock trapped paper under the flap you just made.

31

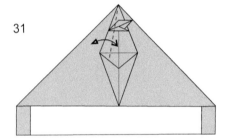

32

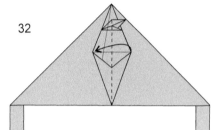

33

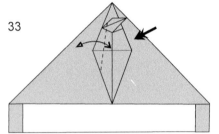

Fold then unfold the side, then repeat steps 30–33 on the other side.

34

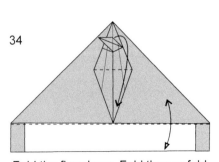

Fold the flap down. Fold then unfold the bottom.

35

36

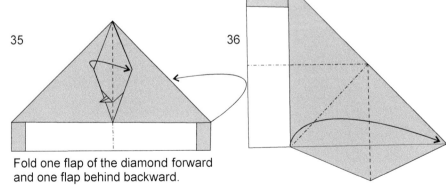

Fold one flap of the diamond forward and one flap behind backward.

Petal fold the flap over, repeat behind.

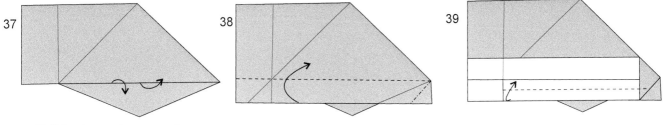

37 Pull the trapped paper out.

38 Squash fold the layer up.

39

40 Inside reverse fold the corner in and out.

41 Return the model to step 38.

42 Repeat steps 38–42 behind.

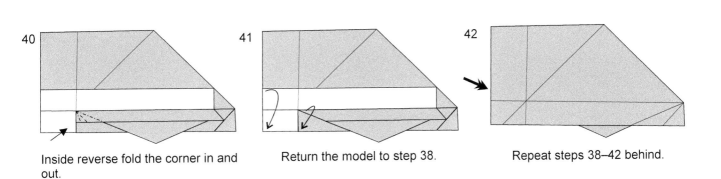

43 Outside reverse fold the paper using the crease.

44 Perform a double swivel fold by swinging the bottom flap down and the top corner down.

45 Turn the model over.

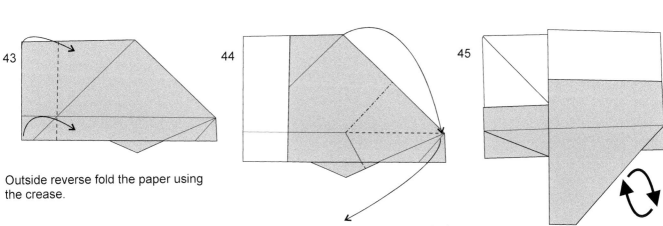
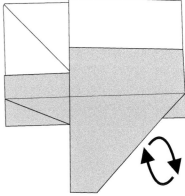

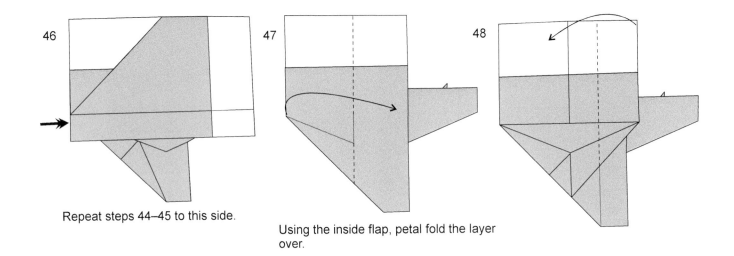

46 Repeat steps 44–45 to this side.

47 Using the inside flap, petal fold the layer over.

48

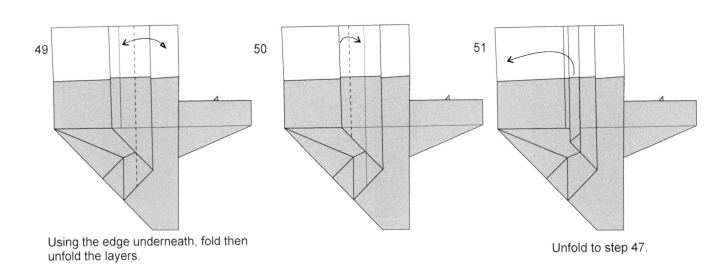

49 Using the edge underneath, fold then unfold the layers.

50

51 Unfold to step 47.

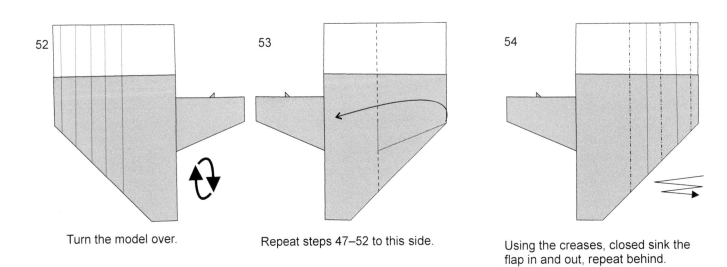

52 Turn the model over.

53 Repeat steps 47–52 to this side.

54 Using the creases, closed sink the flap in and out, repeat behind.

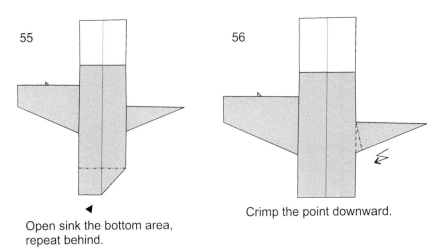
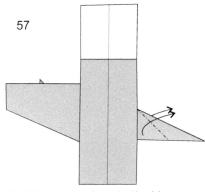

55

Open sink the bottom area,
repeat behind.

56

Crimp the point downward.

57

Pull the layers from both sides up.

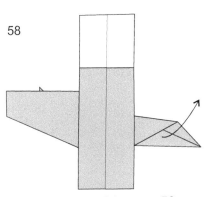
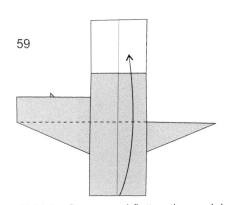
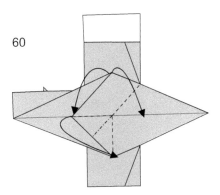

58

Return the model to step 56.

59

Fold the flap up and flatten the model.

60

Squash fold the bottom triangle and
swivel the sides out.

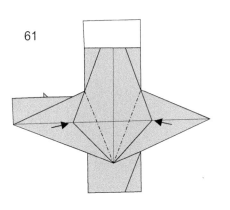
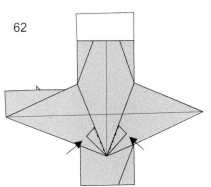
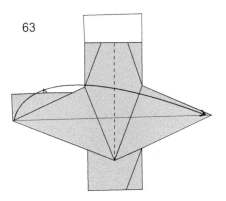

61

62

63

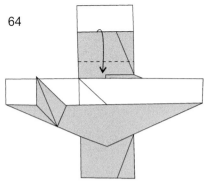

64

Fold the layers down. Note you will have to partially spread it out.

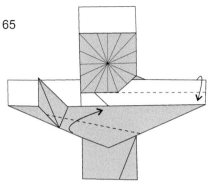

65

Swivel fold the edge down. Fold the bottom edge up.

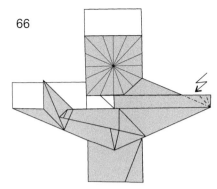

66

Inside reverse fold the corner in and out using the creases.

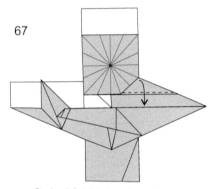

67

Swivel fold this edge down.

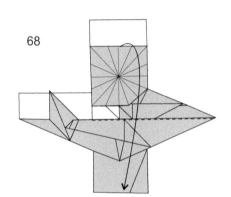

68

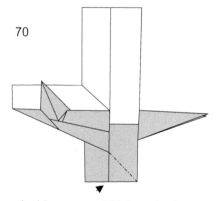

69

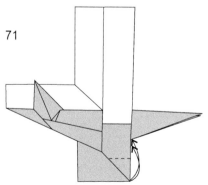

70

Inside reverse fold the edge in.

71

Fold both layers up to the intersection shown.

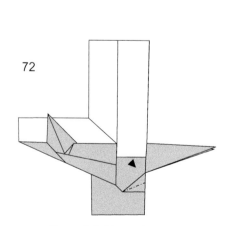

72

Squash fold one layer.

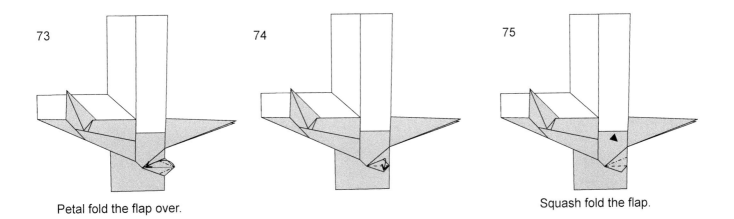

73 Petal fold the flap over.

74

75 Squash fold the flap.

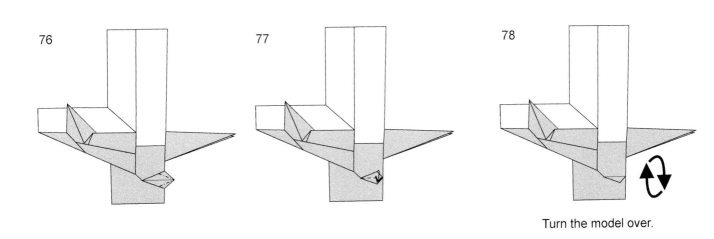

76

77

78 Turn the model over.

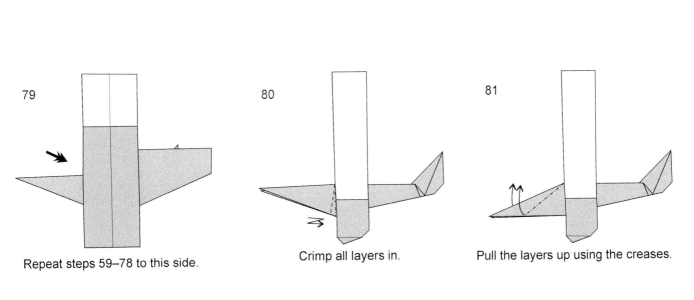

79 Repeat steps 59–78 to this side.

80 Crimp all layers in.

81 Pull the layers up using the creases.

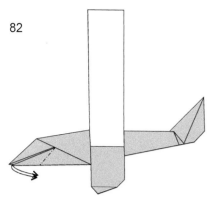

82

Inside reverse fold the flap down, repeat behind.

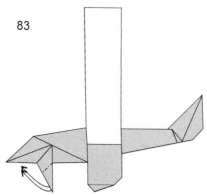

83

Inside reverse fold the flap up, repeat behind.

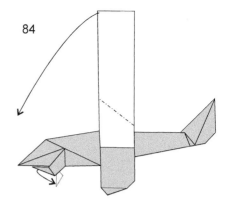

84

Inside reverse fold the large rectangular flap down, swivel fold the small flap out, repeat behind.

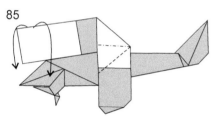

85

Swivel fold the area down on both sides.

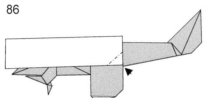

86

Inside reverse fold the small corner in as shown, repeat behind.

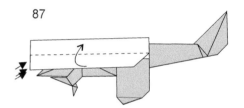

87

First closed sink all of the pleats on the inside, then valley fold the outer layer up.

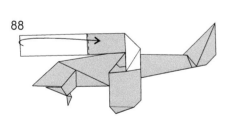

88

Spread the pleats out evenly front and back, then lay the model so it is resting on the pleats. The next series of steps will focus on the pleats.

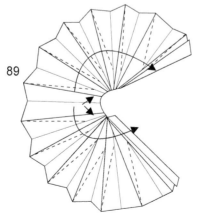

89

Push in the middle of the assembly and flatten out the pleats in the direction shown.

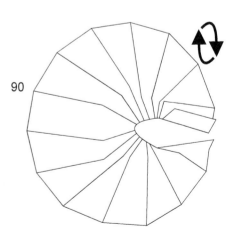

90

Turn the model over.

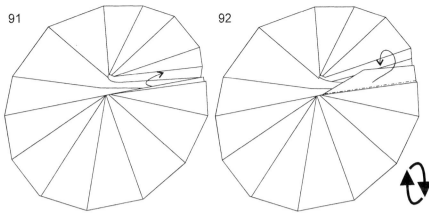

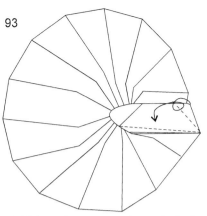

91

Swivel fold the layers up.

92

Mountain fold the edge into the pocket behind it, then turn the model over.

93

Fold the edge over and over to lock the pleats together. Then turn the model so the side faces you. Note the whole model will be shown for the remainder of the steps.

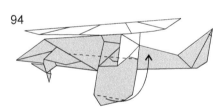

94

Fold the wings up, then fold the hard points down as shown in step 95. Inside reverse fold the tip of the tailfin in.

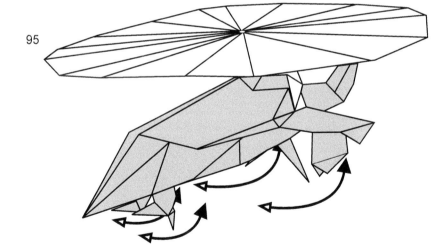

95

You can hide the landing gear by inside reverse folding the rear landing struts and by swivel folding the forward landing struts back into the cannons.